A Vulnerable World

The High Price of Human Trafficking

Elise Graveline Hilton

ACTONINSTITUTE

A Vulnerable World: The High Price of Human Trafficking

Cover images: According to artist Pamela Alderman: "The Scarlet Cord reveals the deception that enslaves innocent children.... This dark world crosses religious and social economic borders to sell our children for sex. A twisting scarlet cord depicts the trauma bond that connects the children to their traffickers." Alderman was inspired, in part, by the story of "Sweetie," found on page 35 of this monograph.

Alderman's art is part of the permanent collections in eleven Children's Hospitals from Philadelphia to San Diego. In 2014, during ArtPrize (the world's largest international art competition, which is held annually in Grand Rapids, Michigan) visitors voted The Scarlet Cord into the Top 25 installations.

ISBN: 978-194250303-3

ACTONINSTITUTE

98 E. Fulton
Grand Rapids, Michigan 49503
Phone: 616.454.3080
Fax: 616.454.9454
www.acton.org

Printed in the United States of America

Contents

Preface

According to the story of creation, "God created mankind in his image; in the image of God he created them; male and female he created them" (Gen. 1: 27). In God's image we were created. This is the source of our dignity and our worth. It also means that each one of us is created to *live free* and to *enter a relationship* with God and fellow human beings. Human slavery, then, has no part in God's plan for human beings.

In our time, however, there exists human trafficking—an estimated 20.9 million modern-day slaves. It is a horrific crime against the fundamental rights and dignity of the human person. The United Nations Protocol on Human Trafficking defines it as "the recruitment, transportation, harboring or receipt of persons by means of force, fraud or coercion."

Traffickers lure vulnerable men, women, and children with false promises of good jobs, an education, economic security, and even love. Once lured, the traffickers are able to keep their victims from seeking help by confiscating identification documents; using threats of violence against the victims or their families; and subjecting the victims to physical, psychological, and/or sexual abuse. There are times that traffickers, instead of luring, actually kidnap children and adults and then force them to do things against their will. No sector or industry is immune from human trafficking. Victims have been identified in factories, restaurants, construction work, agricultural fields, hotels, spas, nail salons, and even private residences.

This modern-day slavery is such a serious issue that Pope Francis in his first Apostolic Exhortation wrote:

> I have always been distressed at the lot of those who are victims of various kinds of human trafficking. How I wish that all of us would hear God's cry: "Where is your brother?" (Gen. 4:9). Where is your brother or sister who is enslaved? Where is the brother and sister whom you are killing each day in clandestine warehouses, in rings of prostitution, in children used for begging, in exploiting undocumented labour? Let us not look the other way. There is greater complicity than we think. The issue involves everyone! This infamous network of crime is now well established in our cities, and many people have blood on their hands as a result of their comfortable and silent complicity. (Pope Francis, *Evangelii Gaudium*, no. 211)

The pope's wish is for all men and women of good will to hear the cry: Where are our brothers and sisters who suffer in this modern day of slavery? For the wish—namely, that all people be sensitized toward human trafficking—to become a reality, all of us need to be educated about this problem. Indeed, to be educated on human trafficking as an offense against fundamental human dignity is the first step on the way to an end to this modern-day slavery.

The author of this book has a passion for eradicating human trafficking. Thus, she has put forth the effort to educate herself about the subject and what to do about it. I consider it a privilege to write the preface for this publication that came from the heart of one of my own parishioners.

In July 2013, I arrived in Cedar Springs, Michigan, to open a brand new parish named after Blessed (later Saint) John Paul II, who was a champion for human rights and dignity. Soon the author of this book and her family joined the new parish. Then, on February 8, 2014, the day that the United Conference of Catholic Bishops prayed for the victims of human trafficking, Elise Hilton sent me an e-mail stating that she would like to make a presentation at the end of Sunday Eucharist on this topic. I quickly agreed to that because this is the topic that I, too, have followed closely since a student at the Gregorian University in Rome (2000–2004). Immediately after the presentation at Sunday Masses, I noticed that she not only had the knowledge but also the passion for the cause. Then one Sunday, I mentioned to her in the Sacristy: "If you write the book, I would love to write the preface." So, here it is: my preface introducing the work of Elise Graveline Hilton who I am very proud to call "my parishioner."

Moreover, I firmly believe that this publication is part of the answer to what Pope Francis said: "Where is your brother or sister who is enslaved?" Let us meet them, let us free them, let us assure them that God loves them and we care for them. First, let us be educated on the issue. Thus, I encourage the people of all faiths, or none, to read this book. May every human being created in the image of God *live free* and *enter a deep relationship* with God and one another.

—Father Lam T. Le

Pastor of Saint John Paul II Parish, Cedar Springs, Michigan, and Mary Queen of Apostles Parish, Sand Lake, Michigan[1]

---

[1] Besides being a pastor, Fr. Lam is an adjunct assistant professor at Aquinas College in Grand Rapids, Michigan. He periodically contributes to theological journals and local newspapers.

1 Introduction

> Human trafficking is an open wound on the body of contemporary society, a scourge upon the body of Christ. It is a crime against humanity. The very fact of our being here to combine our efforts means that we want our strategies and areas of expertise to be accompanied and reinforced by the mercy of the Gospel, by closeness to the men and women who are victims of this crime.[1]
>
> —Pope Francis, Address at a Conference on Human Trafficking, 2014

On January 1, 1863, President Abraham Lincoln issued the Emancipation Proclamation. While it did not entirely end the practice of slavery in the United States, it stands as a symbol to many as the end to the atrocious idea that one human being can own another. Lincoln declared that the American government would recognize and maintain the freedom of all people in the seceded states and that the government would uphold "no act

---

[1] Pope Francis, "Pope Francis: Human Trafficking Is a Crime Against Humanity," *News.va*, April 10, 2014, http://www.news.va/en/news/pope-francis-human-trafficking-an-open-wound-on-so.

or acts to repress such persons, or any of them, in any efforts they may make for their actual freedom."[2]

In the minds and hearts of many, both in the United States and elsewhere, this was the end of slavery. If only that were the case. Slavery, now more commonly known as human trafficking, has not ended. In fact, this human scandal is more extensive than ever.

While human trafficking is not limited to sexual exploitation, the prostitution of human beings is the most lucrative form of trafficking. The canard of prostitution as being the "world's oldest profession" is rejected by journalist Victor Malarek; he calls it the "world's oldest oppression."[3] According to the website of the organization *Free the Slaves*, human slavery was first recorded in 6800 BC in Mesopotamia. The city required slave labor to build and expand. At the height of its so-called glory, the city of Athens was thought to be home to over thirty thousand slaves, and, by 1000 AD, slavery was a normal practice in most of the world. In 1641, Massachusetts became the first British colony to legalize slavery.[4]

Today, human trafficking impacts entire industries and job sectors—both legitimate and illegitimate. Monetarily, it is the second largest criminal activity in the world. Only the illegal drug trade is more profitable—and trafficking and drug smuggling are often linked. The profits generated from human trafficking play an enormous role in national and global economies.

---

[2] Lincoln, Abraham, *The Emancipation Proclamation*, National Archives and Records Administration: Featured Documents, October 15, 2014, http://www.archives.gov/exhibits/featured_documents/emancipation_proclamation/transcript.html.

[3] Malarek, Victor, *The Johns: Sex for Sale and the Men Who Buy It* (Toronto: Key Porter Books, 2010), xiv.

[4] Free the Slaves, "About Slavery: Slavery in History," accessed October 17, 2014, https://www.freetheslaves.net/SlaveryinHistory.

There is also the untold human cost. It is, as Pope Francis said, an open wound on humanity.

Human trafficking is broader in scope than most people realize. To begin, let us define *human trafficking*. According to the United Nations Office on Drugs and Crime, human trafficking is:

> the recruitment, transportation, transfer, harbouring or receipt of persons, by means of the threat or use of force or other forms of coercion, of abduction, of fraud, of deception, of the abuse of power or of a position of vulnerability or of the giving or receiving of payments or benefits to achieve the consent of a person having control over another person, for the purpose of exploitation. Exploitation shall include, at a minimum, the exploitation of the prostitution of others or other forms of sexual exploitation, forced labour or services, slavery or practices similar to slavery, servitude or the removal of organs.[5]

The numbers of people trafficked are almost unfathomable. According to the International Labour Organization, twenty-one million people are trafficked annually;[6] bear in mind that these numbers are estimates. Females and children are most at risk: Over eleven million women are known to be trafficked every year along with five and a half million children (ages eighteen and under). According to Alexis A. Aronowitz, "Women and children are most often the victims of sexual exploitation, followed by sexual exploitation and forced labor combined.

---

5 United Nations Office on Drugs and Crime, "Human Trafficking," accessed October 14, 2014, http://www.unodc.org/unodc/en/human-trafficking/what-is-human-trafficking.html.

6 International Labour Organization (ILO): Geneva, "Profits and Poverty: The Economics of Forced Labour," May 20, 2014, http://www.ilo.org/wcmsp5/groups/public/---ed_norm/---declaration/documents/publication/wcms_243391.pdf.

Men … are more frequently the victims of sexual exploitation and forced labor combined, followed by forced labor and then sexual exploitation."[7]

Sex trafficking gets enormous attention in the academic world and popular culture. Movies such as *Taken* and television dramas such as *Law & Order: SVU* have dealt with this crime. Human trafficking, however, takes many forms. People are trafficked for domestic servitude such as nannying and bonded labor. They are also trafficked for factory work and the mining, agricultural, and fishing industries. Illegal immigration and drug mules also fall under the umbrella of human trafficking. Children are routinely trafficked and forced to beg in the streets or to sell candy and trinkets. Girls are sold as child brides and boys are rounded up to fight as soldiers. Finally, there is cultural slavery, such as in Mauritania, where slavery has existed for centuries, and slave families are routinely handed down to generation after generation of "owners."[8]

In addition, there are the men and women who make their living buying and selling human beings. Some of them, as mentioned, are involved in the highly lucrative drug trade. "Trafficking and smuggling [of drugs and human beings], while different, are in fact intricately intertwined."[9] This type of trafficking is typically part of organized crime. Some traffickers are gang members; others are individuals or loosely affiliated groups of people working together for mutual financial gain. Factory owners, farmers, fishermen: anyone who knowingly utilizes a trafficked person is a trafficker. It must also be acknowledged that corrupt officials (for example, border guards, police, and

---

[7] Alexis A. Aronowitz, *Human Trafficking, Human Misery* (Westport, CT: Praeger, 2009), 37.

[8] Alexis Okeowo, "Freedom Fighter," *The New Yorker*, September 8, 2014.

[9] Aronowitz, 4.

those responsible for licensing bars and restaurants) are an integral part of the chain that holds people in bondage. Sadly, traffickers can also be parents or family members.

Trafficking knows no boundaries. There is no one country that is immune, no demographic that is untouched. Human trafficking is wherever the reader is.

Jerome Elam appears to be an unlikely victim. He is a journalist and a former Marine. Yet his story illustrates that human trafficking is not a crime limited to Southeast Asia or to drug-addicted prostitutes on street corners.

> Following my mother's divorce from my biological father, her life began a downward spiral that left me abandoned and alone, vulnerable to those who prey upon the innocent. My mother's world existed at the bottom of a bottle and when she met a man who began to molest me, alcohol facilitated her complete escape from the reality of what was happening to me. My mother eventually married the man and before long he shared me with the pedophile ring he belonged to. Soon I was being trafficked sexually, trapped by threats of violence against my mother and forced to take cocaine and alcohol.
>
> For seven long years I was trapped in a hell no one deserves. I was nothing more than a shell of a human being enduring suffering and torture at the hands of psychopaths and sociopaths as the world looked on. I attended school, and from the outside appeared to be a "normal child" but I was being trafficked in plain sight. I was often pulled out of school to "service" clients and after school, holidays and weekends were all just a never-ending nightmare for me.[10]

---

[10] Jerome Elam, "The Story of One. Vandalized Innocence: The Story of Trafficked Boys Hidden in Plain Sight," Communities Digital News (CDN), September 20, 2014, http://www.commdiginews. com/life/trafficked-boys-vandalized-innocence-hidden-in-plain-sight-26356/#AbLL85mMbRRrMcxy.99.

It was 1970 in the southern United States; Elam was just five years old when his abuse began.

Why does human trafficking continue to thrive? It thrives because of two of humanity's deadliest sins: greed and lust. It is estimated that human trafficking generates over $150 billion in annual profits, with two-thirds of that from sexual exploitation.[11]

> As we walked in the sand under the blazing sun, MB told me that he operated four brothels in Mumbai, each with approximately four hundred women. He told me his agents bought prostitutes from various places.... Nepal, Bangladesh and other regions of India.... "There is a premium on young girls," MB tells me, "Under fourteen years of age. These girls become very expensive. Sometimes sixty thousand rupees [$1,350 U.S.]." ... MB complained about police payoffs. "This is my biggest expense," he said. MB told me that he rarely visited his brothels, as he spent the majority of his time in the Middle East pursuing business ventures. He claimed he also enjoyed investing in Bollywood films. MB wore several gold chains and had at least four gold teeth. A strict Hindu, he did not eat meat. He did not allow his brothel girls to eat meat either, though copious amounts of alcohol and hashish were allowed.[12]

Experts believe that in the next ten years human trafficking (if left unchecked) will become more profitable to criminals than drugs and arms trafficking and will continue to grow in both developed and developing countries. The purpose of this monograph is to outline both the economic dimension and the moral fallout of modern slavery and to suggest ways that the business of trading in human beings can be severely curtailed.

---

[11] ILO, "Profits and Poverty," 7.

[12] Siddarth Kara, *Sex Trafficking: Inside the Business of Modern Slavery* (New York: Columbia University Press, 2009), Kindle edition.

II Perpetrators and the Business of Human Trafficking

A mother. A fisherman. A factory manager. A restaurant owner. A teacher.

These are the people who traffic in human beings. They buy groceries, drop their kids off at school, hang out at the mall, and belong to clubs and churches. Sure, some of them would make you cross the street if you saw them headed in your direction; however, the most frightening thing about human traffickers is that many look so much like the rest of us.

A case in point: A nineteen-year-old woman from Pakistan, believed to have been born deaf, spent nine years locked in the cellar of a middle-class British home. She was the unpaid housekeeper for the couple who "owned" her, an eighty-five-year-old man and his sixty-nine-year-old wife. The young woman was also subjected to sexual assault from the man. Her life as a slave was an open secret within the family. The couple's forty-seven-year-old daughter was fully aware of her existence and the manner in which she was kept. Upon their conviction, the couple was ordered to pay the victim £100,000 or about $161,000.[1]

---

[1] BBC News, "Cellar Slave Girl: Salford Couple Must Pay Victim £100,000," October 15, 2014, http://www.bbc.com/news/uk-england-manchester-29559771.

For every story like this, there are millions more. For every stomach-churning detail, there is another, far worse.

This chapter will examine the business of human trafficking. First, we will consider the factors that make trafficking possible. Next, we will explore the economic aspect of trafficking and how it affects the legitimate economic sphere. Finally, we will analyze the traffickers themselves. Who are the ones who buy and sell human beings?

The Factors That Make Human Trafficking Possible

There are many factors that create the environment in which human trafficking thrives. These are often referred to as "pull" factors—those attractive circumstances or qualities that pull people into the business of human trafficking and make it possible. The foremost pull is money. If it were not the profit-making machine that it is, trafficking would not exist. As noted earlier, human trafficking creates estimated profits of over $150 billion a year. A single sex-trafficking victim can bring in about $22,000 annually.[2] The profits of different forms of trafficking are estimated at:

- $51.2 billion from forced labor (such as construction or factory work)
- $8 billion from domestic servitude (cleaning and nannying, for instance)
- $99 billion from sexual exploitation

Selling humans has a significant advantage over selling other types of "merchandise." For instance, when a drug dealer sells

---

[2] International Labour Organization (ILO), "Profits and Poverty: The Economics of Forced Labour," May 20, 2014, http://www.ilo.org/wcmsp5/groups/public/---ed_norm/---declaration/documents/publication/wcms_243391.pdf.

his drugs they are gone; used up. The dealer must make or buy more. A human being, however, can be used or sold over and over again for years. When that human being is "done," there are plenty more to choose from.

Human trafficking is a low-cost, low-risk venture with a very high demand, which means large profits. The International Labour Organization, in its "Profits and Poverty" report, has this grim warning:

> The fact that, with limited deterrence, huge profits can be made from millions of poor and uneducated workers provides a compelling argument for stronger government intervention and social and economic development. Despite enhanced enforcement action against forced labour and human trafficking in recent years, it remains a low risk and high gain enterprise. This has to change.[3]

In the 2010 documentary, *The Dark Side of Chocolate*, journalist Miki Mistrati investigates the world of child labor trafficking in Africa's Ivory Coast cocoa industry. While Mistrati was undercover, one plantation owner confided: "If you tell my brother how many children you want, he can get them for you" at the price of about 230 euros (a bit less than $300 US) for each child. The children handle machetes, are exposed to pesticides and the elements and rarely receive any pay. Some are kidnapped into the work. Others are lured from their homes by promises of money. According to the International Cocoa Organization, sales from the ten top chocolate producers topped $86 million in 2013.[4]

---

3 ILO, "Profits and Poverty," 47.
4 International Cocoa Organization, "The Chocolate Industry," February 4, 2014, http://www.icco.org/about-cocoa/chocolate-industry.html.

British reporter Chris Rogers investigated the trafficking of women for sexual exploitation. Working undercover, he established a false Internet company called EUrotica. Traveling to the Czech Republic, he was told he could rent women for six months. The rental price was £5,000 for each woman; £3,000 paid up-front and the remainder when the women were delivered. The women's earnings would be split between Rogers and the Czech traffickers. Rogers told CNN that "within two hours of launching his website, [it] had received 400 bookings."[5] In a two-week period, he could have made £20,000 (approximately $32,000 US) even if only half of the 400 bookings sold.

How much traffickers actually earn remains an admittedly murky area. After all, they are not reporting their earnings to any government agencies. "Even when traffickers are arrested, it is a technical and time-consuming task to uncover the criminal['s] earning[s]."[6] The best estimations remain just that—estimations.

Another determining factor in making trafficking possible is that traffickers face little risk of legal retribution. According to the U.S. State Department's 2014 Trafficking in Persons Report, fewer than 10,000 cases of trafficking were prosecuted worldwide in 2013 resulting in only 5,776 convictions. In 2006, there were 3,160 convictions.[7] Compare that to the 21 million known trafficking victims.

The next consideration is the easy and relatively low-cost travel in our modern world. Even factoring in trafficking expenditures such as forged documents, it costs little to transport a victim

---

5   Alexis A. Aronowitz, *Human Trafficking, Human Misery* (Westport, CT: Praeger, 2009), 64.

6   Aronowitz, *Human Trafficking*, 63.

7   U.S. Department of State, "Trafficking in Persons Report 2014," accessed October 23, 2014, http://www.state.gov/j/tip/rls/tiprpt/2014/?utm_source=NEW+RESOURCE:+Trafficking+in+Persons+R.

across borders, and sometimes even this minimal cost can be bypassed. For instance, India and Nepal have an "open" border so traffickers can easily move victims from one country to another. In *The Dark Side of Chocolate*, Mistrati learned that traffickers simply avoid official border checkpoints and use unsecured back roads to transport the children they are trafficking. Within the European Union, there are more-or-less open borders. It goes without saying that there are no border checks from one state to another in the United States. An organization, Truckers Against Trafficking,[8] also in the United States, works to educate truck drivers to not only recognize possible sex trafficking victims forced to work rest areas and truck stops but also to be alert to traffickers who hire truckers to "move their merchandise."

When it becomes necessary to smuggle victims, traffickers are adept at finding creative ways to get their merchandise from one place to another. A Nigerian man sought travel visas for his female badminton team for a tournament in Europe. Embassy officials were suspicious and upon questioning the young women, found that none of them knew anything about the sport. That trafficker failed in his efforts to use this "legal" method of moving his victims.[9]

Ease of travel has also created an entire industry based on the trafficking of human beings: sex tourism. Thailand, the Philippines, Malaysia, Costa Rica, and Russia are "destination spots" for those seeking sex for money.

> Today sex tourism accounts for half of all visitors to Thailand [where prostitution is actually illegal], with the annual income from prostitution making up between

---

8 Truckers Against Trafficking, http://www.truckersagainsttrafficking.org/.

9 Aronowitz, *Human Trafficking*, 56.

> 10 to 14 percent of the country's gross domestic product—and it is still growing.[10]

While scenes of middle-aged white men trolling bars for young women in order to pay for sex are pathetic and degrading, nothing compares to the horror of the sex tourism involving children. Only one example is necessary to show the depravity of this scenario.

> In June 2006, a U.S. citizen was arrested in Phnom Penh, Cambodia, for allegedly torturing and raping a 20-year-old woman and at least three young girls between the ages of 9 and 11. The 53-year-old offender, Michael Joseph Pepe, was a school teacher. The offender bought one of the children from her mother for $300; the other girls he rented ... for $30 a month.[11]

The almost universal access to the Internet has certainly made the work of a human trafficker easier. Websites such as Craig's List and Backpage allow traffickers to offer their "wares" for free. Ads for massages and models are thinly veiled advertisements for prostitution.

For most of us, the Internet is where we work, correspond with friends, catch up on news, and shop. We do all this on what are known as "surface sites"; sites that are well-known, easily accessible, and legitimate businesses. These surface sites make up only about 4 percent of web traffic. The rest of web traffic takes place in what is known as the Deep Web.

> The Deep Web is made up of dynamic content, or content that is password-protected, unlinked, restricted by form-controlled entry, or updated ahead of search engine

---

[10] Victor Malarek, *The Johns: Sex for Sale and the Men Who Buy It* (Toronto: Key Porter Books, 2010), 137.

[11] Aronowitz, *Human Trafficking*, 135.

indexing. (Imagine an enormous labyrinth with a limitless amount of doors leading into it. But, you don't know where the doors are, what is behind each door, or the code to open any of the doors.) Harmless examples of "dynamic" content include your emails on Gmail, .pdf or .doc files stored on Dropbox, personal information stored on Facebook, or private photo albums from your last family reunion.

The malicious Deep Web content that should concern us is primarily hosted on Tor and .onion peer-to-peer network servers (P2P networks), as well as obscure image sharing websites that can only be accessed if you have specific URLs, usernames and passwords. These areas of the Deep Web are where proactive action needs to be taken to stop the largely undeterred child predators who are trading child pornography or offering children for sale.[12]

The anonymity of the Internet is a cloak that hides much suffering at the hands of human traffickers.

By far, the most important component for making human trafficking possible is corruption. From paying off a border guard to look the other way, to an entire government (such as Thailand's) ignoring the booming-yet-illegal sex industry, corruption makes trafficking possible and profitable.

> Corruption of government officials leads to the moral and legal deterioration of a government which could result in additional criminal activities on the part of corrupt officials. Furthermore, States may actually be complicit in situations where structures or officials facilitate trafficking, turn a blind eye or create obstacles to improving or passing legislation, or arresting and prosecuting traf-

---

[12] Raymond Bechard, "What You Must Know About the 'Deep Web,'" Examiner.com, April 25, 2014, http://www.examiner.com/article/what-you-must-know-about-the-deep-web.

fickers. In this sense, the State violates victims' rights and becomes an offender.[13]

The corruption that facilitates trafficking can take nearly benign forms such as paying a government inspector to hasten the licensing of a bar. At other times, the corruption extends to those who are supposed to lend aid and enforce the law, which turns them into an insidious part of the trafficking web.

Siddarth Kara, while investigating sex trafficking in Rome, Italy, had a conversation with a young Polish woman who had been promised a modeling career and ended up being prostituted.

> Later that night, I asked the street unit team "Is it not illegal for minors to engage in prostitution, even if they say they choose to?"
>
> "Yes," they replied.
>
> "Then why don't the police assist them? Why don't they prosecute the protectors for pimping the minors?"
>
> "The police are the main clients," I was told.[14]

A study in Malaysia traced a network of corruption that enabled traffickers to bring victims into the Philippines with relative ease, including so-called officials who would escort traffickers and their victims through customs "with little or no documentation."[15] The study also uncovered police corruption; high-ranking officers enjoyed free drinks and the services of

---

[13] Alexis Aronowitz, Gerda Theuermann, and Elena Tyurykanova, *Analysing the Business Model of Trafficking in Human Beings to Better Prevent the Crime*, Organization for Security and Co-operation in Europe (OSCE), May 2010.

[14] Siddarth Kara, *Sex Trafficking: Inside the Business of Modern Slavery*" (New York: Columbia University Press, 2009), Kindle edition.

[15] Aronowitz, *Human Trafficking*, 62.

prostitutes in return for allowing bars and strip clubs to remain uninvestigated.

International Justice Mission, a Washington, DC, based NGO, has discovered that in many parts of the world, people in need of police and/or legal assistance "often actively *avoid* these systems because they are so abusive."[16] The Michigan Commission on Human Trafficking also addressed this issue by noting that impartial application of the law is necessary for a stable society and that

> organized crime, political corruption, other ancillary illegalities associated with trafficking impede law enforcement efforts, slow economic growth and undermine public trust.[17]

Countries that lack rule of law not only allow trafficking to thrive, but they discourage victims from coming forward. In fact, victims are often retraumatized by their attempts to get help from government officials who either simply do not care or are paid not to. Without the rule of law, victims—past, present, and future—have no legal redress.

To recap, factors that make trafficking an easy and attractive business are the enormous amounts of money to be made, the relative wealth much of the world has to spend, the ease of travel, and the lack of legal retribution. In addition, easy accessibility to the Internet and widespread corruption make human trafficking less complicated and more profitable.

---

[16] International Justice Mission, *Justice Review: A Journal on Protection and Justice for the Poor, 2014–2015* (September 2014): 7.

[17] Michigan Commission on Human Trafficking, "2013 Report on Human Trafficking," 17.

The Economic Aspects of Human Trafficking

The profits of human trafficking affect legitimate economies in significant ways. One of the first things that must be admitted is that consumers who are horrified by the idea of human trafficking may quickly balk at prices of everyday products in a world without trafficking. Most of us want to be moral but many will turn a blind eye to ethics if the price difference on an item is significant enough. Anti-Slavery International, reporting on slave labor in India, says,

> It is ... clear ... that a significant pressure on cost reduction comes from the procurement practices of international businesses, which emphasise low cost and fast delivery above labour conditions.... Producers seek the means to meet production demands at low cost in a globally competitive environment, where there is a constant fear of losing out to manufacturers in other lower cost countries.[18]

Many of us unwittingly enjoy the fruits of trafficking labor. We go out for dinner, enjoy a hotel stay during a family vacation, shop frugally at stores featuring low prices, and take our children to a small-town carnival. All of these are instances where our lives come into possible contact with human trafficking victims. One victim, who was brought into the United States by way of legal venues for a nanny job and suffered three years of abuse by her "employers," stated, "These people work

---

[18] Anti-Slavery International, "Slavery on the High Street: Forced Labour in the Manufacture of Garments for International Brands," June 2012, 22, http://www.antislavery.org/includes/documents/cm_docs/2012/s/1_slavery_on_the_high_street_june_2012_final.pdf.

jobs that cushion our lives with comfort; we're all benefiting from their exploitation and may not even realize it."[19]

The global supply chain is a complex system. What consumers see as a simple trip to the store to pick up family necessities is not as straightforward as putting an item in a shopping cart, paying for it, and taking it home. There is a vast array of people and processes that put each item on a store shelf; many of them are touched by people who are trafficked. As one analyst observes:

> As consumers continue to demand less expensive goods, food and services, firms in developed countries have struggled to cut costs and increase profits, particularly during the international recession. Because labor is one of the greatest costs to a firm, some firms are willing to employ trafficked victims in order to maximize their profits. Businesses that employ trafficked victims pay them very little, if at all, and require long work hours and high quotas. Victims also must endure poor and dangerous working conditions.[20]

At a purely economic level, labor trafficking creates an unfair playing field. For those who choose to utilize trafficked workers, their bottom line stays artificially low. In order to compete, honest businesses must find legitimate ways to lower prices for consumers, find consumers who are willing to consistently pay higher prices, or be driven out of business. Legitimate businesses are subject to taxes and levies; illegal businesses are not.

---

[19] Tanvi Misra, "How the Crime of Labor Trafficking Helps Cities Run," *Citylab*, October 21, 2014, http://www.citylab.com/crime/2014/10/how-the-crime-of-labor-trafficking-helps-cities-run/381709/.

[20] Anna Fletcher, "Human Trafficking within the Global Supply Chain," *Sigma Iota Rho Journal of International Business* (April 30, 2014).

One writer calls the relationship between legitimate and illegitimate economies (such as human trafficking) "symbiotic."[21] For instance, in the textile industry the underground economy is tightly interwoven with the legitimate one. The textile industry may boast high-fashion clothing, beautiful models, and glossy magazine spreads, but it also scuttles along in the dark with overworked, underpaid, and unpaid laborers who are subjected to dangerous and often fatal conditions.[22] The strands of both legal and illegal business become woven together: Where does one start and the other end?

We must also take into account the cost of treating survivors. Richard J. Gelles and Staci Perlman[23] have done extensive research in the area of child abuse and neglect in the United States. While they do not specifically focus on victims of trafficking, we can extrapolate from their findings. Gelles and Perlman calculate that the direct cost of child abuse and neglect (for example, the cost of law enforcement, legal costs, and so forth) exceed $33 billion annually. Indirect costs (housing, education, and mental health) exceed $46 billion annually. We would have to multiply these costs to include adult survivors and the global landscape to get a truer picture for human trafficking, but it is clear: These are costs that affect all of us directly.

---

[21] Aronowitz, *Human Trafficking*, 33.

[22] Jim Yardley, "Report on Deadly Factory Collapse in Bangladesh Finds Widespread Blame," *New York Times*, May 22, 2013, http://www.nytimes.com/2013/05/23/world/asia/report-on-bangladesh-building-collapse-finds-widespread-blame.html?_r=0.

[23] Richard J. Gelles and Staci Perlman, *Estimated Annual Cost of Child Abuse and Neglect* (Chicago: Prevent Child Abuse America, 2012).

Supply and Demand

There are many experts who attempt to understand human trafficking from a purely business model. In this case, there is supply (the victims) and demand (the traffickers.) When studying money and human trafficking, we cannot simply leave the discussion at the profits made by criminals. We must also consider that we live in a time of great wealth. While there is dire poverty, there are also many in the modern world with a great deal of disposable income. While one man may indulge his passion for motorcycles, another uses his income to visit Costa Rica eight times in three years to bed prostitutes.[24]

In the business of sex trafficking, those who create demand are the "johns." These are (primarily) the men who, for a variety of reasons, seek out sex for pay. In *The Johns: Sex for Sale and the Men Who Pay for It*, Canadian journalist Victor Malarek writes about the variety of reasons men pay for sex. Some claim loneliness and the inability to create normal relationships. Others have a deep hatred of women, which plays out in their using women merely as sexual objects. Yet others are pathological predators. Regardless of why men choose to hire prostitutes, Malarek says, "It is time to stop looking at johns as a faceless footnote to what is now increasingly recognized as a very serious social problem. Men are the drivers behind prostitution."[25]

Then we have the middlemen—the recruiters. These are the people who lure others into trafficking. While most recruiters in the world of sexual exploitation are men, there are also women who recruit.

Imagine, for example, a fourteen-year-old girl who hangs out at the mall. Like many teens, she feels misunderstood by her parents. She may, in fact, be neglected at home; her mother

---

[24] Malarek, *The Johns*, 143.

[25] Malarek, *The Johns*, 14.

has a new boyfriend and younger children with him, and the teenage girl has become an afterthought. She is often burdened with caring for her younger siblings and finds refuge at the mall.

A man, just a bit older, strikes up a conversation with her. He tells her he knows just how she feels; he has been through the same thing. He makes her laugh and tells her how pretty she is. Hungry for attention, she allows her guard to drop. When he suggests that the two get something to eat, she agrees. Over a meal, he again tells her how pretty she is and offers to buy her some clothes or makeup. Once the purchase is made, he tells her that she should not have to deal with that old cell phone she has; he buys her a top-selling model, telling her it will be "their way" of communicating. The girl may not know it, but she has just been lured into the world of sex trafficking.

Because many teens are wary (as they should be) of a strange man at the mall, pimps often use women to recruit. These are typically women who have worked for the pimp for a while, are trusted in their organization, and are crudely known as "bottom bitches." These women often use the same routine as described above: They befriend lonely and isolated girls, luring them in with gifts and the promise of an understanding older friend. In return, the older women often get gifts and money from the pimp as "rewards" for their loyalty. Recruiters are true predators; they study and stalk their prey as well as any beast.

Carissa Phelps, in her autobiography *Runaway Girl: Escaping Life on the Streets*, describes a childhood of chaos. Ten siblings, little money, and an unpredictable and violent stepfather were the realities of her everyday existence. When her older sister warned her that their stepfather was trying to sell off their virginity, Carissa left to live with her father. Life there was quieter, but she was introduced to pornography, which no doubt "lowered her resistance" to sex at a young age. Inexplicably, she became homesick and returned to live with her mother and stepfather.

While Phelps was good at school, her home life became an unhealthy whirlwind of running away and coming home. She learned that sex was the price she had to pay for food and a place to stay for the night. By the age of twelve, she was under the "protection" of a pimp. "You're going places, girl," he told her, "I'm gonna take care of you."[26] Carissa was not necessarily lured into sex trafficking so much as she fell into it as a form of survival.

Labor Trafficking

Those who traffic in sex often work alone or in a loosely organized group of like-minded people, but in labor trafficking, the situation is, by necessity, a more organized effort.

The Urban Institute's report, "Understanding the Organization, Operation and Victimization Process of Labor Trafficking in the United States,"[27] is a terrific boon for those working to investigate the complex world of trafficking. Here, we see that traffickers must work in conjunction with many others in order to get the labor they seek. There are, amongst other roles, recruiters, transporters, supervisors, business owners, and subcontractors.

In an infamous case of trafficking in California, Trans Bay Steel, Inc., recruited forty-eight men from Thailand as welders. While the company provided visas for the men, their visas and passports were taken away from them when they arrived in the States. One man, desperate for work, borrowed $12,500 from

---

[26] Carissa Phelps, *Runaway Girl: Escaping Life on the Streets* (New York: Viking, 2012), Kindle edition.

[27] Urban Institute, "Understanding the Organization, Operation, and Victimization Process of Labor Trafficking in the United States," October 21, 2014, http://www.urban.org/publications/413249.html.

the company against his $200 promised monthly wage for a "recruitment fee."[28]

The men were promised housing, which they received: run-down apartments with no gas, electricity, or furniture. Complaints were met with threats of sending them back to Thailand with no money. Some of the men were "lent out" to a Thai restaurant, working thirteen-hour days and sleeping on the floor. One of the workers was able to escape, which resulted in an unusually happy ending.

> In one of the most comprehensive awards in recent history, the company is required to pay the workers relocation expenses to Napa, California. They will also train and certify the workers as welders.
>
> The company will also pay for tuition and books at a local college for the unskilled workers to train as welders. The company agreed to guarantee minimum pay and a base pay once the claimants complete their training period.[29]

Siddarth Kara says that the business model of trafficking is simple. There are "four components: a product (the victim), a wholesaler (the trafficker), a retailer (the slave owner/exploiter), and a consumer."[30] Yet nothing in the realm of human trafficking is simple, and the case above illustrates this. There were at the very least dozens of people both in the United States and in Thailand who were fully aware of the situation these men were

---

[28] Aronowitz, *Human Trafficking*, 46.

[29] *Labor Law Center Blog*, "California Company Convicted of Slavery and Human Trafficking," August 7, 2007, http://blog.laborlawcenter.com/news/california-company-convicted-of-slavery-and-human-trafficking/.

[30] Kara, *Sex Trafficking*, chap. 8, Kindle edition.

in. Many people had the opportunity to make things right; not one of them did so until forced to by a court.

Trafficking at this level requires sophisticated plans. However, there is (according to Alexis Aronowitz) "little evidence of highly structured, hierarchical organized crime enterprises involved in human trafficking."[31] Rather, these alliances tend to be loosely organized, opportunistic, and fluid. The business of human trafficking, it seems, is comprised mainly of small-business owners; the Trans Bay Steel case seems to be more exception than rule.

There is, unfortunately, an economic "upside" to trafficking for consumers: It keeps prices low on commonly purchased items. This is one reason that awareness of human trafficking is so important. Consumers need to be able to make informed decisions about how and what they purchase. Human trafficking damages the finances of legal businesses and ties up money in criminal activities that could otherwise be used legitimately.

Another matter to consider is that law enforcement and court and penal systems spend a great deal of time and money on victims. If they were able to see victims of trafficking as true victims (a prostitute is a victim, especially if they are under the age of eighteen), they would pursue the traffickers. That is where the money is. Imagine if every man in the United States who purchased sex was made to pay substantial fines and court fees, and those fines could be used to help treat victims. The economics of trafficking would certainly change. Both awareness of the crime of trafficking and willingness on the part of government officials to pursue traffickers are necessary for positive change, both economically and legally.

---

[31] Aronowitz, *Human Trafficking*, 66.

Human Traffickers: Who They Are and the Tactics They Use

By this point, one can see that there is a wide range of people involved in the trafficking of human beings. From the stereotypical pimp who has several prostitutes "working" for him to large companies that utilize slave labor, it is obvious that there is no one face of a human trafficker. Perhaps the only things traffickers have in common are their lack of compassion and empathy and their willingness to trade human lives for profit.

Alexis Aronowitz has a helpful list of types of traffickers. Although it does not include the smallest trafficking operations where one or two people are the mainstay of the operations, it is fairly comprehensive.

- Investors
- Recruiters
- Transporters
- Corrupt Officials and/or Protectors
- Informants
- Guides and/or Crew Members
- Enforcers
- Debt Collectors
- Money Launderers
- Support Personnel[32]

Most of these are self-explanatory but a few require unpacking. A protector is someone who is not there to protect the victim but rather to protect the trafficker's investment. The protector is the one who makes sure that a victim is cleared through customs, is hidden away from prying eyes of neighbors, and so forth. A guide is paid to help a trafficker move victims across borders and away from secure checkpoints. A debt collector is

---

[32] Aronowitz, *Human Trafficking*, 68.

the person in a larger organization who makes sure that money flows up the chain from lower-rung personnel to those higher up in the organization. Support personnel might be someone local who provides transportation, food, housing, and/or logistics for a limited period of time.

The trafficker is nearly as likely to be female as male, at least in the world of labor trafficking. In sex trafficking, the trafficker is still overwhelmingly male: In the Urban Institute's study, "Estimating the Size and Structure of the Underground Commercial Sex Economy in Eight Major US Cities," all of the convicted pimps interviewed were male. In labor trafficking, it appears that men are the traffickers only about 68 percent of the time.[33] Traffickers (or at least those arrested for trafficking) tend to be in their thirties and forties.

While it may be difficult to create a picture of a "typical" trafficker, it is not hard at all to get an idea of how they operate. The types of control techniques are almost universal. In sex trafficking, young people are often recruited through "soft" control as described earlier. As mentioned before, an older man or woman finds a vulnerable young person, for example, and gives them attention, affection, and gifts. Another common technique is promising a job such as being a nanny or a model in another country, thus luring the young person away from home. In time, the situation changes. Sometimes, the victim is told, "You owe me; you need to start earning some money after all I spent on you." Other times, the threats are more overt. In addition, sex-trafficking victims are not only at risk of violence from those trafficking them but also from those who purchase their services.

Another form of control used by traffickers is to frequently move victims so as to disorient them. In regions like the EU, victims may be moved to places where they do not speak the

---

[33] Urban Institute, *Understanding the Organization*, 41.

language in order to further control them. In domestic servitude situations, a victim may have virtually no control over her movements. She may not be allowed outside the house, or is allowed out only when supervised by a family member.

Victims are demeaned and demoralized. Sex-trafficking victims are often "broken in" by being raped repeatedly by the trafficker and/or others in their circle. Victims may have all their personal belongings taken away. Their ethnicity may be cause for taunting, and they may constantly be the victims of verbal abuse. One can imagine how terrible it would be—especially to a child—to undergo a constant barrage of verbal abuse, especially when in unfamiliar and frightening circumstances.

Victims of trafficking may be controlled by violence, threats of violence to their family members, and threats that they will be deported even if they are able to escape. They are told that the police will not help them (and sadly, in many cases, this is true.) Victims may also be controlled with drugs, alcohol, sleep deprivation, and food deprivation.

Traffickers are predators. They hunt and kill human souls. They feel no guilt in selling a teenage girl for sex dozens of times in one night or kidnapping a man as slave labor in a foreign land, never for him to return home. They are violent, manipulative, corrupt, and often quite wealthy. They are the mothers next door, the businessmen across the street, and the men in the mall. They are all around us, seeking prey.

III   Victims and "Push" Factors

No little girl dreams of working in a dimly lit bar having sex with dozens of men night after night. No boy envisions for himself a life of harvesting cocoa pods, with no shelter for sleep, far from home, not knowing if he will ever escape this slavery. No man wants to be so desperate to feed his family that he trusts a stranger with his life and his "debt money," only to find himself in a foreign country, working for no pay and little food, knowing that his life is in the hands of monsters.

This is the world of the victims of human trafficking. Some have been duped, some kidnapped, and others sold by family members. Some believe they have no choice but to trust a promise too good to be true in order to escape oppressive poverty. No one freely chooses a life of brutality, slavery, or rape—a life where one is no longer seen as human but merely an object to be sold and used.

If we want to address human trafficking effectively, we must first understand the climate that produces its victims. What are the factors that create the vulnerability described above? What are the factors that "push" a human being into slavery? How do we weaken or eliminate these push factors?

Poverty, Globalization, and Trafficking

Without a doubt, the single largest push factor for human trafficking is poverty. Dire poverty, as *The Economist* notes, makes for a life that not only lacks the most basic necessities but also fits the Hobbesian caricature of "nasty, brutish and short."[1] In that same article, however, we are given reason to hope: Over the past twenty years, nearly one billion people have been lifted from extreme poverty.

The secret to the alleviation of poverty is no secret at all, according to Samuel Gregg. He says that those blessed with wealth need to be generous, but we must also utilize the opportunities created by business owners and entrepreneurs, who are "focusing upon what they know how to do—which is to create wealth—and by alerting others to the conditions that enable business to create wealth, employment and better living standards for all."[2]

Others, however, blame the global landscape (instead of poverty) for human trafficking. Anna Fletcher, writing in the *Journal of International Business*, explains:

> One of the worst consequences of globalization is human trafficking. With liberalized trade and firms constantly searching for inexpensive labor and goods, globalization has increased the likelihood that the most vulnerable and already exploited citizens, mainly children and those in

---

[1] "Towards the End of Poverty," *The Economist*, June 1, 2014, http://www.economist.com/news/leaders/21578665-nearly-1-billion-people-have-been-taken-out-extreme-poverty-20-years-world-should-aim.

[2] "Recipe for Ending Poverty: Think, Then Act," Zenit.org, November 30, 2009, accessed October 23, 2014, http://www.zenit.org/en/articles/recipe-for-ending-poverty-think-then-act.

extreme poverty, will be trafficked into forced labor, debt bondage, or the sex industry.[3]

What is "globalization"? Has it indeed created the grim world described above?

Lord Brian Griffiths, international advisor to Goldman Sachs and former senior policy advisor to Margaret Thatcher, defines globalization as "the increasing integration or interconnectedness of nations through increased trade, investment and the migration of labor."[4]

Put this way, globalization appears to be morally neutral. In this regard, Gregg writes:

> Globalization allows for more trade, more cross border movement, etc. In a sense, that may make human trafficking easier. But the issue of globalization versus closed economies is actually irrelevant when it comes to the *cause* of human trafficking. Human trafficking is ultimately *caused* by people *freely choosing* to treat others as objects. The fact that it is easier to cross borders in a globalized world makes human trafficking easier, but that in itself is not the cause. And does anyone doubt that even if we had closed economies, human trafficking would still occur? Of course it would. We would have women and children being *smuggled* across borders.[5]

Janie Chuang from the Washington College of Law disagrees:

---

[3] Anna Fletcher, "Human Trafficking within the Global Supply Chain," *Sigma Iota Rho Journal of International Business*, April 30, 2014.

[4] Lord Griffiths of Fforestfach, *Globalization, Poverty, and International Development: Insights from* Centesimus Annus (Grand Rapids: Acton Institute, 2012), Kindle edition.

[5] Samuel Gregg, e-mail message to author, September 15, 2014.

The problem of trafficking begins not with the traffickers, themselves, but with the conditions that caused their victims to migrate under circumstances rendering them vulnerable to exploitation. Human trafficking is but "an opportunistic response" to the tension between the economic necessity to migrate, on the one hand, and the politically motivated restrictions on migration, on the other.[6]

Is globalization the beast responsible for the scourge of human trafficking?

It is not. Chuang's assessment denies human moral agency and holds that people are essentially animated by circumstance. Thus, she removes responsibility from those who exploit others, saying, in essence, "Globalization made me do it."

Saint John Paul II offers this perspective:

The trade in human persons constitutes a shocking offence against human dignity and a grave violation of fundamental human rights. Already the Second Vatican Council had pointed to "slavery, prostitution, the selling of women and children, and disgraceful working conditions where people are treated as instruments of gain rather than free and responsible persons" as "infamies" which "poison human society, debase their perpetrators" and constitute "a supreme dishonour to the Creator" (*Gaudium et Spes*, 27). Such situations are an affront to fundamental values which are shared by all cultures and peoples, values rooted in the very nature of the human person.[7]

---

[6]   Janie Chuan, "Beyond a Snapshot: Preventing Human Trafficking in the Global Economy," *Indiana Journal of Global Legal Studies*, January 2006, http://www.repository.law.indiana.edu/ijgls/vol13/iss1/5/.

[7]   John Paul II, Letter of John Paul II to Archbishop Jean-Louis Tauran on the Occasion of the International Conference "Twenty-First Century Slavery—The Human Rights Dimension

We cannot and must not blame the victim, lessen the responsibility of the trafficker, or simply shrug our shoulders and say that globalization is at fault. Even in the most dire of circumstance, each of us is a free and morally responsible person. However, every person requires the right conditions to be able to develop a fully mature conscience and thus make sound moral decisions. Many human trafficking victims (and in some cases, traffickers) have not been allowed such circumstances. Of course, many people *do* assent to sin and criminal activity with a fully informed conscience.

With this in mind, we ask, "Is globalization a push factor in trafficking?" Globalization and trafficking exist, but there is no evidence to prove that the former causes the latter.

Poverty and Human Trafficking: It Is Not Just Money

We know what causes poverty, and, as Gregg states above, we know how to fix it—we are just not doing enough of it. Over the past fifty years, the overarching policy to "fix" poverty in the developing world has been foreign aid, and that has been a dismal failure. Herman Chinery-Hesse, a software entrepreneur in Ghana, states, "I don't know of any country in the world … where a bunch of foreigners came and developed the country. I don't know one: Japan? Korea? No! No country did that."[8] For similar reasons, the War on Poverty in the United States has not achieved its goals either.[9]

---

to Trafficking in Human Beings," May 15, 2002, http://www.vatican.va/holy_father/john_paul_ii/letters/2002/documents/hf_jp-ii_let_20020515_tauran_en.html.

[8] Herman Chinery-Hesse, "Business vs. Aid & Charity," Poverty-Cure.org, accessed October 29, 2014, http://www.povertycure.org/voices/herman-chinery-hesse/.

[9] Robert Rector and Rachel Sheffield, "The War on Poverty After 50 Years," The Heritage Foundation, September 15,

Poor people are not stupid; they are poor. However, poverty is not simply a lack of money. It is a lack of education and a lack of rule of law to protect property rights and fair legal access for all. It is discrimination against females or certain ethnic groups. It is corruption, and it is the continuing barriers that exist to free-trade policies. Given better economic and educational choices, human trafficking would (at least for many) lose its appeal.

It is also clear that the breakdown of sound cultural norms and the traditional family structure leads to both moral and financial impoverishment. In *Walking Prey: How America's Youth Are Vulnerable to Sex Slavery*, Holly Austin Smith, a trafficking survivor, asserts that she was "primed" for trafficking—not by global markets or dire poverty, but by pop culture. She says, "In elementary school, I wanted to be an archeologist like Indiana Jones or a gymnast like Mary Lou Retton. By intermediate and middle school, however, I was enamored with Hollywood."[10] She goes on to quote a former San Diego District Attorney: "We live in a society [in which] a child cannot avoid constant exposure to sex as a vehicle for selling something." For Smith, this translated into selling her body in order to obtain the material possessions she craved.

It must be made clear in the fight against human trafficking that poverty can mean not only a lack of money but also a lack of moral guidance, a lack of sound family structure, a lack of protection against cultural norms that devalue the person, and a lack of responsibility on the part of anyone who sees or takes part in immoral activity and chooses to do nothing to better

---

2014, http://www.heritage.org/research/reports/2014/09/the-war-on-poverty-after-50-years.

[10] Holly Austin Smith, *Walking Prey: How America's Youth are Vulnerable to Sex Slavery* (New York: Palgrave-MacMillan, 2014), Kindle edition.

the situation. Unfortunately, this type of poverty is far more difficult to alleviate than is financial poverty.

One illustration of cultural impoverishment is in Albania where women have traditionally been devalued. In many cases, a woman's hope rests on securing a decent man to care for her. Her other choice, a cultural tradition that appears to be dying out, is to choose to "become" a man in a common-law ritual known as *virgjinesha*, or sworn virgin. After taking a virgin oath, the woman effectively is transformed into a man (without any surgery or hormone treatments). She dresses as a man and is recognized socially as male. Women generally choose this if they have no marriage prospects or if their parents lack male children. While this custom is becoming more rare, it points to the fact that women are of little "value" in Albanian culture. If a woman is not married or does not become a man, she is likely to become destitute, especially if she has no father or brother to care for her.[11] For too many women, in Albania and elsewhere, economic, educational, and social choices are severely limited.

Siddarth Kara, in his global travels to research sex trafficking, saw first-hand how this type of cultural confinement leads to trafficking in Albania. He recounts what one Albanian woman, Pira, told him of her experience:

> This man named Alban proposed marriage when I was seventeen. We had a wedding ceremony in my village. I remember dancing with my younger sister. After the wedding when I moved to my husband's home, he sold me for one hundred thousand leke [$1,000] to another man. That man took me by truck to Kosovo. We crossed the border by foot. I was forced for sex in a club one year before a police raid. When I returned to my home, I

---

[11] Siddarth Kara, *Sex Trafficking: Inside the Business of Modern Slavery* (New York: Columbia University Press, 2008), Kindle edition.

> learned Alban married two other women and sold them
> also. The same priest conducted the ceremonies.[12]

This is a sad illustration of the communal aspect that creates some human trafficking situations. Clearly, there is an enormous amount of collusion here: the young man, the priest, and others who not only knew but conspired. Trafficking does not take place in a vacuum. Many people know and choose to either participate in or ignore the evil.

Albania has also become an international marketplace for human organs, and children are an appealing source of them for traffickers. Many—perhaps thousands—of trafficked Albanian children end up in Greece. While some children are used as domestic servants or are forced to beg, others face something far worse. Parents often sell their children into the organ trafficking world because the lure of money seems to justify the risk for the desperate. Victims of organ trafficking may be kidnapped and forced to give up an organ against their will, they may be tricked (told they will receive a certain sum of money, which they do not), or they may be told—falsely—that they have a medical issue that requires the removal of an organ.[13]

The fact that parents sold their children was confirmed when Kara was told "that the majority of children trafficked to Greece were sold or sent willingly by parents." The official with whom Kara spoke told him that trying to rescue trafficked children was dangerous work. The official said he had been warned by a judge on the International Criminal Court: "Work on child trafficking for sexual exploitation, begging, what have you. Work

---

[12] Kara, *Sex Trafficking.*

[13] Andy Brienzo, "Trafficking for Organ Trade: The Often-overlooked Form of Human Trafficking," *Human Trafficking Center Blog*, June 18, 2014, http://humantraffickingcenter.org/posts-by-htc-associates/trafficking-organ-trade-often-overlooked-form-human-trafficking/.

on child trafficking for organ harvesting, and you're dead." Kara continues: "Organs such as kidneys, livers, and hearts can be sold for thousands of dollars, making the traffic in child organs just as lucrative as sex trafficking is."[14]

In many parts of the world, females suffer the most when it comes to violence. They are the first to be trafficked, the most likely to be physically abused, and the most likely to be kidnapped or killed. The April 2014 abduction of the Christian schoolgirls by Islamic extremists in Nigeria highlights this very danger. Even infants are not safe. "Sweetie," too young to even walk, was tied to a post with a scarlet cord to keep her from crawling off as her seventeen-year-old mother was forced to prostitute herself on the streets of India. Sweetie's future remains unclear; her only hope is that she will be rescued from the fate that has befallen her mother.[15]

World Vision UK, in the report "Untying the Knot: Exploring Early Marriage in Fragile States," confirms that girls in many parts of the world are at risk for early marriage (as young as the age of nine), and suffer from systemic cultural inequalities, violence, and a lack of education. While some families view marriage at a young age as a form of protection for their daughters, others hold girls in so little esteem that they are no more than baggage that must be off-loaded to prevent further economic drain.

In Vietnam, young women are sold as "brides" for Chinese men for as little as $150. This typically occurs in market settings.[16] Young women over the age of eighteen are considered "unmarriageable" and are sometimes auctioned off. Typically,

---

[14] Kara, *Sex Trafficking*.

[15] "Sweetie," Women at Risk, International, accessed November 4, 2014, http://warinternational.org/story/sweetie/.

[16] Kara, *Sex Trafficking*.

these women never do marry because they are taken to China to work in the sex industry.

Boys and men living in dire poverty do not fare much better. One of the vilest forms of trafficking is in the Asian fishing industry, which relies heavily on young boys for labor. It is not unusual for boys to be taken to sea for months at a time where they are forced to work almost around the clock for no pay. Many of the boys lose their lives—not all accidentally—in these dangerous conditions. Kara describes the connection between slavery and the seafood industry:

> Countless lives are extinguished at the end of the fishing runs, so that profits for wholesalers remain high and prices for fish-hungry consumers remain low. Beyond the fishing, forced labor tactics are used throughout the supply chain, from processing to packaging of seafood for distribution throughout the West, most prevalently in the $1.5 billion shrimp markets of Bangladesh and Thailand.[17]

Again, in the business of human trafficking, the supply is abundant and cheap. The deaths of a dozen young boys are nothing more than an inventory issue, easily resolved.

Lest we believe that labor trafficking is something that takes place only in Bangladesh sweatshops or Thai fishing boats, the Urban Institute has clearly documented abundant labor trafficking in the United States. Strikingly, the majority (71 percent) of victims of labor trafficking in the United States enter the country legally.[18] Most are males who are trafficked

---

[17] Kara, *Sex Trafficking*.

[18] Urban Institute, "Understanding the Organization, Operation, and Victimization Process of Labor Trafficking in the United States," October 2014, p. 24, http://www.urban.org/UploadedPDF/413249-Labor-Trafficking-in-the-United-States.pdf.

in the agricultural industry. While sex trafficking victims tend to be young (the average age of a person entering the realm of sex trafficking is twelve), labor trafficking victims are generally adults. In the Urban Institute study, the average age of the victims when they entered the trafficking market was thirty-three. This study also reveals that many victims are trafficked at the hands of family members.

> One interviewee … left her home country when she was a minor and moved to the United States to live with a family member who would ultimately be the perpetrator of her labor trafficking victimization. The survivor believed that her family members residing in her home country, many of whom had encouraged her to move to America, were knowledgeable of the exploitative situation that awaited her in the United States. Similarly, another survivor was recruited and trafficked by her aunt.[19]

Most victims in this study said that poverty and violence in their home countries were strong push factors—conditions that left them vulnerable to trafficking.

While economic poverty is devastating and is an evident push factor in human trafficking, it is also clear that cultural and educational poverty (especially for women) leads to trafficking.

Can Fixing Poverty Help End Human Trafficking?

There is evil in our world. There will be evil in our world until the end of time. Good people will always strive to dispel evil but will never be able to eradicate it completely.

That said, good people can and must do everything in their power to create fair, just, and equitable systems for all. If poverty is one of the driving factors behind human trafficking, we

---

[19] Urban Institute, "Understanding the Organization," 49.

must work to diminish poverty as much as possible in a world marked by sin.

We bear in mind the words of Christ Jesus: "The poor you will always have with you" (Matt. 26:11). There will always be those who, for whatever reason, cannot care for themselves, or who find themselves in temporary circumstances that require assistance from those around them. It is our responsibility to care for those who cannot care for themselves and to help those in situations more transitory in nature.

There are those who are entrenched in extreme economic poverty and all the issues that surround it: educational inadequacies, health issues, pressure to migrate, and the violence that seems all too often to accompany poverty. We have the ability to ease these situations. How do we go about it?

PovertyCure is an initiative launched in 2011 that addresses these very issues. In an interview for PovertyCure, Fr. Robert A. Sirico, a leading thinker on the intersection of ethics and the economy, said, "Business is the normative way in which people rise out of poverty, not state-to-state aid, not the largesse of politicians and bureaucrats."[20] Sirico goes on to say that we must make sure that the parameters for success are set: "When markets can expand within a juridical framework, with an ethical system at the center, the poor can rise out of poverty and have access to goods, to services, to employment, and to all of the things that a prosperous society can afford."[21]

Although neatly summed up in a few sentences, this is an enormous task. It will require radical changes on the part of government and civil agencies here and abroad as they seek to address poverty—a distinct alteration of what compassionate

---

[20] Rev. Robert A. Sirico, "The Moral Case for Business," "Voices," PovertyCure, accessed November 5, 2014, http://www.povertycure.org/voices/rev-robert-a-sirico/.

[21] Sirico, "Voices," PovertyCure.

aid means and a response from the private sector to create long-term, sustainable strategies that increase jobs and wealth while decreasing the economic lure of trafficking.

C. Neal Johnson, author of *Business as Mission: A Comprehensive Guide to Theory and Practice*, knows the value of work. Having a job does not simply mean food on the table or money to buy necessities. Work has transformative power:

> One of the problems we saw in Kazakhstan when I was on the mission field there was that the people didn't have jobs. The men were out, they didn't think well of themselves so what did they do? They turned to the bottle; alcoholism problems were really rampant. They're angry, they're frustrated, they have no hope in life, and they don't see any value in their life. But you take that same person, you give them a job, you give them something meaningful, and it can totally change their attitude toward life and gives them hope, gives them promise.... So business not only creates valuable goods and services, but we're creating employment for people that allows them to have a whole different sense of who they are, what their purpose is, and what their hope is for the future. And the social implications of that are just enormous.[22]

Now think back to Siddarth Kara's description of life for women in Albania and rural Vietnam. Imagine the possibilities for change, not just in income, but in true renewal of families and culture.

Business has the ability to transform lives of poverty not just into *productive* lives but also into *flourishing* ones.

According to the World Bank, Haiti is the poorest country in the Americas. One of the few businesses that thrives is human

---

[22] C. Neal Johnson, "Spiritual & Social Aspects of Business," "Voices," PovertyCure, accessed November 5, 2014, http://www.povertycure.org/voices/c-neal-johnson/.

trafficking: "Haiti is a source, transit, and destination country for men, women, and children subjected to forced labor and sex trafficking."[23] Despite the abundance of foreign aid lavished on Haiti in recent decades, poverty remains the norm.

Corrigan and Shelley Clay found themselves in this environment in 2007.[24] The Canadian couple traveled to Haiti hoping to adopt an orphan, but the Clays' plans quickly changed when they realized that most of Haiti's orphans have parents who simply cannot afford to feed and educate their children. Parents turn children over to orphanages out of desperation.

In response, the Clays decided to move to Haiti and create a for-profit business, the Apparent Project (a PovertyCure partner.) The company's website describes the Clays' vision:

> At the Apparent Project, we believe that the best way to alleviate the tragic effects of poverty is to help the poor create wealth. In our work in Haiti we are particularly interested in providing job opportunities for parents. If the root cause of poverty is not addressed, thousands of kids are at risk for growing up in institutions. Jobs are the easiest, most sustainable, most straightforward, natural and dignified way to overcome this problem. Job creation empowers the poor to be the solution to the problems that confront them.[25]

Since 2007, the Clays have created artisan associations where adults are taught skills such as jewelry-making and pottery. Their

---

[23] U. S. Department of State. "Trafficking in Persons Report 2014." Accessed October 23, 2014. http://www.state.gov/j/tip/rls/tiprpt/2014/.

[24] Mindy Belz, "From the Works of Their Hands," *WORLD Magazine*, February 22, 2014, http://www.worldmag.com/2014/02/from the_work_of_their_hands.

[25] Apparent Project, "Job Creation," accessed November 6, 2014, http://www.apparentproject.org/job-creation/4575497652.

creations are sold in the global marketplace. The artisans are given the dignity of work, the opportunity to learn skills that provide for their families, and the ability to raise themselves from poverty.

This is the type of response to poverty that we need. As Sirico observed, business is the way people escape poverty; creating wealth through legitimate business is the answer to dire poverty. If we, as a global community, are able to utilize the force of business, entrepreneurship, and human innovation, then we can continue to move people out of extreme poverty and into lives of dignity and prosperity.

Rule of Law and Human Trafficking

It does a person little good to start a business if she cannot prove she owns the land it sits on. Worse is the case where she can prove it, but someone with more power simply takes it from her, and she has no legal recourse due to corruption and the lack of rule of law.

What is "rule of law?" In his seminal book, *Natural Law and Natural Rights* (1980), Oxford legal philosopher John Finnis argued that legal systems embody the rule of law to the extent that (1) their rules are prospective rather than retroactive, (2) their rules are not impossible to comply with, (3) their rules are promulgated, (4) their rules are clear, (5) their rules are coherent with respect to each other, (6) their rules are sufficiently stable to allow people to be guided by their knowledge of the content of the rules, and (7) those charged with the authority to create law are accountable for their own compliance and to consistently administer the law.[26]

---

[26] John Finnis, *Natural Law and Natural Rights* (Oxford: Clarendon Press, 1980), 270.

Among other things, this means that all citizens be accorded the same rights under the law and be held equally responsible for their actions. It covers everything from a speeding driver getting a ticket—whether he is a judge or a janitor—to crime victims receiving protection *by* the police and not *from* the police. There is not one set of rules for some and another set of rules for others. Rule of law levels the playing field for all citizens. The law applies to all equally.

A *lack* of rule of law means that those with the most money and power win. It means that corruption among government officials is unchecked. It means that victims of crimes who are poor or have no political and legal connections have little or no recourse.

Political and legal corruption in Nepal means that people are easily trafficked across the open border to India. Tiny Hands International, an NGO, works in Nepal to raise awareness regarding human trafficking in both the public and legal sectors and has created after-care programs for survivors.

At the 2014 Interdisciplinary Conference on Human Trafficking at the University of Nebraska-Lincoln, Tiny Hands International researcher Andy Brienzo presented the organization's simple, effective method for working within a corrupt system in order to stem the flow of trafficking victims.[27]

Tiny Hands trains local Christians who volunteer at major transit hubs and border crossings between India and Nepal. These people are taught to spot potential trafficking victims and question them if need be. The workers might ask potential victims if they know where they are going in India, for example,

---

[27] Andy Brienzo and Jonathan Hudlow, "Fighting Human Trafficking through Transit Monitoring: A Data Driven Model Developed by Tiny Hands International," (paper read at the Interdisciplinary Conference on Human Trafficking University of Nebraska-Lincoln, October 10, 2014).

or what type of work they will be doing. They might ask if they have had to pay anyone for the job. Tiny Hands also relies on what Brienzo called "high value contacts" such as rickshaw and bus drivers for information regarding traffickers.

Because corruption in Nepal is so prevalent, Brienzo explained, Tiny Hands has learned to work with officials without getting caught in the web of corruption. By gathering evidence, Tiny Hands is able to hand over enough information to the police in some trafficking situations that the police have their case essentially built for them. The police get credit for catching traffickers, victims are rescued, and no money changes hands.

Tiny Hands' use of locals is important for several reasons. The police and possible victims tend to be more trusting of their fellow countrymen than of "outsiders." The volunteers are also able to quickly spot things that seem to be out of place, such as the color of clay on someone's shoes or a particular native dress, which might be clues that a person is from a region where traffickers tend to recruit.

Given the culture of corruption, one wonders if the locals who work with Tiny Hands are at risk of "being bought." Tiny Hands president and founder John Molineaux responds:

> We feel confident that our subcommittee members do not accept bribes for the simple reason that they are volunteers whose lives are regularly threatened. If money and personal benefit were what they were after, they would not be risking their lives without compensation on behalf of the innocent victims of trafficking.... We hear about our staff and subcommittee members being offered bribes frequently, but we have never heard an allegation that any of our staff or subcommittee members have taken a bribe.[28]

---

[28] John Molineaux, e-mail to author, October 15, 2014.

International Justice Mission (IJM) has done compelling and successful work in the area of rule of law as well. Cambodia, a nation that had an entrenched sex industry, has seen success with the work of IJM.

> In the early 2000s, Cambodia was well-known as an international haven for sex tourists where pedophiles could sexually abuse children with impunity. Emblematic of the rampant violence against very young children was Svay Pak, a neighborhood 11 kilometers outside of Phnom Penh, where girls as young as five were readily available in shacks lining the streets for foreigners to purchase for sexual acts. The police were complicit in the trade, receiving bribes for not arresting [the] brothel owners and pimps who were openly violating Cambodian law.[29]

Thankfully, the situation today is drastically different. With much hard work, the trafficking of minors has been substantially reduced, and the legal system has been transformed. IJM took several steps to make this happen. After Cambodia created the Anti-Human Trafficking and Juvenile Protection unit in 2002, IJM partnered with local law enforcement in Svay Pak to rescue more than thirty victims and to successfully prosecute traffickers and brothel owners.

In 2004, IJM opened an office in Phnom Penh as their long-term headquarters in that country. IJM has lawyers, investigators, and social workers who cooperate with local authorities to find and rescue victims, while helping to build cases against traffickers. IJM also works with local organizations that provide victims with long-term recovery services.

Throughout 2012 and 2013, IJM, along with external partners, worked to measure "the prevalence of commercial sexual exploitation of children … in Phnom Penh, Siem Reap and

---

[29] "International Justice Mission," *Justice Review* (2014–2015): 21.

Sihanoukville, Cambodia."[30] Bearing in mind that trafficking is hard to measure given its hidden nature, the results of the study remain quite encouraging. The study found that not only had the prevalence of minors (especially those under the age of fifteen) in the sex industry dropped substantially but also that law enforcement was far better trained to investigate trafficking cases and to interview both victims and traffickers. The resources available to law enforcement are more substantial now than fourteen years ago, and the public perceives the police to be far more trustworthy in the fight against trafficking.

In addition, judges and prosecutors in Cambodia are growing more knowledgeable about human trafficking, and Cambodia continues to improve its after-care services for trafficking survivors.

The work IJM has done in Cambodia, as well as in places such as Guatemala, the Philippines, and Uganda to strengthen the rule of law and equip those charged with enforcing the law with knowledge and tools, should be a source of great hope for those involved in fighting human trafficking.

The United States: Rule of Law and Woeful Ignorance

What about the United States? Does the rule of law here have bearing on the fight against human trafficking? While the United States enjoys far better rule of law than most of the world, there are still many areas regarding trafficking where improvements must be made.

The Urban Institute is blunt: "[l]ocal police do not understand what human trafficking is. They ... do not believe it is something they would encounter in the normal course of their duties."[31]

---

[30] "International Justice Mission," *Justice Review*, 22.

[31] Urban Institute, "Understanding the Organization," 165.

One law enforcement officer, working surveillance, assumed that because the victims had bicycles, they could not be victims:

> They had bicycles at the house. They were free to go to the store.… They spent most of their waking hours at the restaurant working, but on the few afternoons that they would have off, they could do whatever they wanted.[32]

Clearly, the officer in question had never been taught that trafficking victims often do not speak the local language, may be fearful of police and possible deportation or may have no idea where they are, because they are moved frequently.

Another case is even more frustrating. One woman, a victim of domestic servitude in the United States, was actually able to call 911 for help … or so she thought. When the police arrived, the homeowner first tried to tell the police that it was a mistake; no one had called 911. When the victim spoke up, saying she had been physically assaulted, the homeowner/trafficker denied the assault. The police left, but only after they told the victim she could go to jail for falsely calling 911.

Several questions are raised by this account:

> [W]hy would law enforcement choose to believe the story of the individuals who did not make the emergency call? Moreover, even if the officers believed the word of the trafficker, wouldn't the safest scenario have been to remove the individual who made the call from the situation?… Finally, and most disturbingly, why would a member of law enforcement threaten any individual with incarceration for using emergency systems?[33]

Of continued frustration for those working to end human trafficking is the manner in which victims are treated by police

---

[32] Urban Institute, "Understanding the Organization," 77.

[33] Urban Institute, "Understanding the Organization," 96.

in many situations. For instance, the State of Michigan's 2013 Report on Human Trafficking found that the Michigan State Police do not even recognize human trafficking as a crime, unless it involves a homicide or kidnapping.[34]

This type of woeful ignorance on the part of law enforcement regarding existing laws and of human trafficking itself means that victims are often treated like criminals. Holly Austin Smith was not even in high school when she was arrested for prostitution. At the police station, handcuffed to a bench, she was yelled at by one police officer to "sit like a lady."[35] When her parents arrived, they were not quite sure what to do with her, as she had been a habitual runaway. The cop roared that he was not a babysitter and to "get her the hell out of my station."

Smith was briefly hospitalized, then taken by detectives to see if she could identify the hotel where she had been held and interrogated. "Nearly twenty years later," she writes:

> I obtained a copy of that interrogation and it still pains me to read it. I remember the officer questioning me, and I especially remember him addressing me as *Miss Smith*. Here are my problems with this scenario: I was a *child*. I was being interrogated in an unfriendly environment, by myself, with two unfamiliar male detectives, and one of them spoke to me like I was an adult. I'm often asked what would have helped here—a female detective? A different room? A victim advocate? And, my answer is *yes*! All of the above! Appointing one officer in charge of cases involving child victims of commercial sexual exploitation would be most helpful, though, especially one who is trained to handle such cases. The officer's matter-of-factness with me made me want to pick up my

---

[34] State of Michigan, *2013 Human Trafficking Commission Report*, 21.

[35] Smith, *Walking Prey*.

> chair and throw it at him. Nobody *talked* to me like I was
> a person outside of a criminal case. I felt like an alien.[36]

To be clear, in the United States, no child is a prostitute under the law. Anyone under the age of eighteen who is found to be involved in commercial sexual activity is always and only a victim.[37]

It would be nice to look at Smith's experience and say, "That was twenty years ago. Certainly, police work in the United States regarding trafficking and victim-services has improved?" That would be overly optimistic.

Shared Hope International released "Demanding Justice" in 2014. The introduction states: "America's youth are at a risk because of a simple economic principle—demand for sex acts with children drives the market of exploitation."[38] Shared Hope wants child victims of trafficking to receive necessary and needed services and wants to see adult buyers of child sex acts brought to justice. The "Demanding Justice" report investigates what stands in the way of those two goals.

The following is a telling scenario:

> Police in Las Vegas approached a parked truck after observing it pick up a girl. The police report reflects that the 50-year-old man was observed with $45 in cash hanging from his pocket and lotion on his hands. The 12-year-old girl stated that he was paying her for sexual services.

---

[36] Smith, *Walking Prey.*

[37] United States Department of Justice, "Child Exploitation & Obscenity Section," accessed November 7, 2014, http://www. justice.gov/criminal/ceos/subjectareas/prostitution.html.

[38] Shared Hope International, *Demanding Justice Report 2014*, 4, http://sharedhope.org/wp-content/uploads/2014/08/Demanding_ Justice_Report_2014.pdf.

The police arrested the girl for prostitution and sent the man on his way.[39]

One can interpret this as the police removing a minor from a dangerous situation, but they could do that without arresting the minor. The fact that the man was not arrested, however, is inexcusable. (By the way, prostitution is illegal in Las Vegas—even for adults.)

In one discussion recounted in the "Demanding Justice" report, a state legislator noted that typically, those who buy sex are "ordinary" guys: "husbands, fathers, business leaders—not the type of people we usually associate with criminal conduct; as a result, prosecuting them makes people feel uncomfortable."[40]

In other words, prosecuting a seedy hooker or a thuggish pimp is much more palatable. Changing this viewpoint will take two things: (1) holding accountable those who buy and sell human beings, and (2) treating victims *as* victims, not as criminals. The former requires rule of law; the latter requires a cultural shift.

"Send 'em back!" Immigration and Migration Issues

Far too often victims of human trafficking end up in foreign countries: unable to speak the language, unfamiliar with the culture, and unequipped to even prove they are who they say they are because they lack documentation. Even if they had proper legal immigration status on entering a foreign country, it is likely they no longer have the documentation. Taking victims' visas, passports, and other credentials is one way that traffickers are able to control them.

Thus, if the person is able to escape the trafficking situation in a foreign country, they have legal issues. They may also have a safety issue if they are sent back to their country of origin:

---

[39] Shared Hope, *Demanding Justice*, 19.
[40] Shared Hope, *Demanding Justice*, 37.

Will they likely be retrafficked if they return to the environment where they were trafficked in the first place?

In studying labor trafficking in the United States, the Urban Institute found that the vast majority of those trafficked were here legally. Some wished to return home, but 14 percent were jailed for being unauthorized immigrants rather than being recognized as victims of trafficking. Imagine being held hostage by a trafficker for years and finally finding freedom. Then, you are imprisoned for a crime you did not commit. "Although the labor trafficking survivors ... who were arrested and placed in jail and/or deportation proceedings by immigration officials eventually received immigration relief, the trauma and revictimization they experienced cannot be [overstated.]"[41]

The U.S. Immigration and Customs Enforcement, along with Homeland Security, have developed a status known as "Continued Presence" or CP. This is

> a temporary immigration status provided to individuals identified by law enforcement as victims of human trafficking. This status allows victims of human trafficking to remain in the U.S. temporarily during the ongoing investigation into the human trafficking-related crimes committed against them. CP is initially granted for one year and may be renewed in one-year increments.[42]

Christian Organizations Against Trafficking in Human Beings (COATNET), a network of thirty-six Christian organizations (Catholic, Protestant, and Eastern Orthodox), is committed to finding ways to end trafficking. On the issue of

---

[41] Urban Institute, "Understanding the Organization," 130.

[42] U.S. Immigration and Customs Enforcement, "Continued Presence: Temporary Immigration Status for Victims of Human Trafficking," August 2010, http://www.ice.gov/doclib/human-trafficking/pdf/continued-presence.pdf.

migration/immigration, they have a sensible approach. They believe that nations should:

> [offer] secure shelter for trafficked persons in the countries of destination, transit and origin (for repatriated trafficked persons); [thus] providing individual social, medical, psychological, and legal assistance, as well as vocational training to empower trafficked persons professionally. Effective assistance requires trans-national cooperation and networking ... effective assistance should also pay particular attention to the spiritual healing of the trafficked persons and to their full spiritual and mental rehabilitation, in order to enable them to deal with the lifelong suffering that invariably is caused by trafficking.[43]

The National Council of Jewish Women, which has an excellent track record of supporting anti-trafficking legislation, agrees with this approach and reminds us that it is important for victims to be able to testify in legal cases:

> Rather than being returned to their home countries, victims must be able to remain in the United States during any criminal or civil proceedings against their abusers. Victims must be guaranteed immunity from prosecution of immigration laws or other crimes deriving from their victimization. And those who fear retaliation if they are deported must also be permitted to apply for permanent resettlement in the US.[44]

---

[43] COATNET, "The Caritas Internationalis Commitment on Combating Trafficking in Human Beings," October 2005, http://www.caritas.org/includes/pdf/coatnet/CI_Commitment-2.pdf.

[44] National Council of Jewish Women, "NCJW Condemns Human Trafficking," December 5, 2005, http://www.ncjw.org/content_3137.cfm.

While government agencies must be involved in issues of immigration, border control, and national security, many of the needs of trafficking victims can and should be met by private agencies. We will discuss this in more detail later. For now, suffice it to say that taking the stance that illegal immigrants suspected of being trafficking victims should always be sent back to their country of origin is shortsighted and inhumane.

Role of Culture in Human Trafficking

In a world where we are taught to be nonjudgmental; to view everyone's cultural norms (however abhorrent) as valuable; and to "coexist," as a ubiquitous bumper sticker says, it must be said that some cultures do not treat women and children well at all—and that drives human trafficking.

Jewish and Christian teaching holds that every human being is created in God's image and likeness and that each "possesses intrinsic value and dignity, implying certain rights and duties both for himself and other persons."[45] There are no exceptions here; every person is included, regardless of gender, age, capabilities, race, or any other qualifier. Unfortunately, not everyone sees this truth.

In the brothels of Mumbai, a girl is sold by her parents for twenty thousand rupees (about $444 US).[46] In Albania, a father trades his seven-year-old son to human traffickers for a used television.[47] In Thailand, many tribal people simply do not

---

[45] Acton Institute, "Acton Institute Core Principles," accessed November 14, 2014, http://www.acton.org/about/acton-institute-core-principles.

[46] Kara, *Sex Trafficking.*

[47] Alexis A. Aronowitz, *Human Trafficking, Human Misery* (Westport, CT: Praeger Publishers, 2009), 21.

exist as far as the government is concerned.[48] In such tribes, if a child is born and his or her birth is not registered with the government within twenty-four hours, that child does not exist. Never mind that government offices may be dozens of miles away. Why bother trying to save a child from trafficking if she does not exist in the first place?

Do not think America is immune from such cultural traps. Becky McDonald, president and founder of Women At Risk, International (WAR, Int'l) in Grand Rapids, Michigan, says, "We sell our babies here," and at the same Acton Institute panel discussion in February 2014, Michigan State Senator Judy Emmons (R.–33rd District), stated, "Traffickers are looking for younger and younger individuals, both boys and girls.… If we don't get a handle on this, our future generations will pay dearly."[49]

Samuel Gregg defines culture as "the choices, beliefs, actions, values, and institutions that shape a society, including its economic arrangements."[50] If this is the case, then culture plays an enormous role in human trafficking. Whether it is the decades-old slave trade that endangers the lives of girls as young as seven in Sundhupalchok, Nepal,[51] or the glorification of the

---

[48] Kara, *Sex Trafficking*.

[49] "Hidden No More: Exposing Human Trafficking in West Michigan," Acton Institute, March 28, 2014, https://www.youtube.com/watch?v=NBYcjT7-0sY.

[50] John Horvat II, The American Society for the Defense of Tradition, Family and Property, "Interview with Dr. Samuel Gregg: 'Culture Drives History, Societies and Economic Life,'" July 28, 2014, http://www.tfp.org/tfp-home/news-commentary/interview-with-dr-samuel-gregg-culture-drives-history-societies-and-economic-life.html.

[51] Kara, *Sex Trafficking*.

pimp culture in American hip-hop,[52] many people choose to believe, act, and value lifestyles that demean women, children, healthy and wholesome family life, and the intrinsically good factors that create a moral culture.

Today, the scales are tipped toward human trafficking. Children of a certain cultural heritage do not exist, women are bought and sold, and people continue to make money from the debasement of other humans. William Wilberforce, the great British abolitionist, said, "God Almighty has set before me two Great Objects: the suppression of the slave trade and the reformation of manners."[53] For Wilberforce (and the society he lived in), "manners" referred to public morality. It is clear that God has set before us these same two objectives.

A Realistic Look at Victimization and Push Factors

This chapter has offered a stark look at the victims of human trafficking and the most prevalent push factors. It is not easy to acknowledge these things. What is worse, though, is to acknowledge poverty, cultural emptiness, despair, issues with rule of law and immigration—and do nothing about them. Pope Benedict XVI stated this well in his 2009 encyclical *Caritas in Veritate*:

> [Globalization] has been the principal driving force behind the emergence from underdevelopment of whole regions, and in itself it represents a great opportunity. Nevertheless, without the guidance of charity in truth, this global force could cause unprecedented damage and create new divisions within the human family. Hence charity and truth confront us with an altogether new

---

[52] Malika Saada Saar, "The Scandal of the Players Ball," The Daily Beast, December 10, 2010, http://www.thedailybeast.com/articles/2010/12/10/players-ball-hip-hop-and-sexual-abuse.html.

[53] Stephen Tomkins, *William Wilberforce: A Biography*" (Grand Rapids: Eerdmans, 2007), 59.

and creative challenge, one that is certainly vast and complex. It is about *broadening the scope of reason and making it capable of knowing and directing these powerful new forces*, animating them within the perspective of that "civilization of love" whose seed God has planted in every people, in every culture.[54]

"Charity in truth" is the measure against which all work to end human trafficking should be measured.

---

[54] Pope Benedict XVI, *Caritas in Veritate*, June 29, 2009, sec. 33, http://www.vatican.va/holy_father/benedict_xvi/encyclicals/documents/hf_ben-xvi_enc_20090629_caritas-in-veritate_en.html.

IV What Is to Be Done about Trafficking?

The fact that we are still talking about how to eliminate the enslavement of human beings in the twenty-first century would certainly confound the likes of Frederick Douglass, William Wilberforce, and Harriet Beecher Stowe. They would likely be horrified that not only does slavery still exist but also that it has spread with epidemic-like force.

We can diminish human trafficking, and we must. The task is enormous, but there is hope.

Solutions to Human Trafficking

Efforts to eradicate human trafficking must be victim-centered. Victims of human trafficking should not be treated like criminals by law enforcement, courts, or immigration officials. Our work must be both proactive and reactive in order to eliminate human trafficking—always with the needs of high-risk populations and victims in mind.

The first step toward eradicating human trafficking is to raise awareness. Very few people know that human trafficking exists and that it exists where they live. People must be told that traffickers are doing business in their communities. "Awareness-raising programmes … are examples of measures taken to reduce the likelihood that victims will come into contact with motivated offenders."[1]

Yet awareness is not enough. Andy Soper, founder of the Manasseh Project (a program designed specifically to treat female teen victims of trafficking) in Grand Rapids, Michigan, cautions about simply raising awareness, saying that we run the risk of turning people from "ignorance to willful apathy."[2] Therefore, the second step toward eradicating human trafficking is that we must educate and equip people to act responsibly.

Knowledge of the signs of human trafficking should be ubiquitous, as are signs of child abuse or domestic violence. Public awareness puts pressure on traffickers, and Polaris Project is an excellent resource on this[3] (see appendix). Organizations such as Polaris Project and Redlight Traffic[4] instruct people on what to do if they suspect trafficking. Medical personnel, first-responders, teachers, and others who would be in positions most likely to come into contact with victims should make it a priority to be educated.

Stephany Powell, executive director of the Mary Magdalene Project (a program that helps women escape prostitution) says that current education about human trafficking is about where we were as a society with domestic violence and child abuse

---

[1] Alexis Aronowitz, Gerda Theuermann, and Elena Tyurykanova, "Analyzing the Business Model of Trafficking in Human Beings to Better Prevent the Crime," (paper presented at the Organization for Security and Co-operation in Europe [OSCE], May 2010), 32.

[2] Andy Soper, "Hidden No More: Exposing Human Trafficking in West Michigan," (Panel at the Acton Institute, March 28, 2014), https://www.youtube.com/watch?v=NBYcjT7-0sY.

[3] Polaris Project, "Recognizing the Signs," accessed November 18, 2014, http://www.polarisproject.org/human-trafficking/recognizing-the-signs.

[4] Redlight Traffic, http://www.redlighttraffic.org/.

thirty years ago.[5] A report analyzing the business aspect of trafficking states:

> Any time initiatives are taken to raise awareness of potential victims or customers of trafficked persons, this raises the cost and risk to traffickers. When expertise is developed among agencies investigating situations involving exploitation, this increases the risk to this business. Increased prosecution will raise the risk and increase costs to traffickers, while asset seizure and confiscation will reduce profits. Most of these measures, taken together, provide governments with tools to attack the business of human trafficking.[6]

Siddarth Kara[7] has several suggestions for being proactive in the developing world. One is similar to the program by Tiny Hands International discussed earlier. It would train community committees, taxi drivers, business owners, and others to gather information and work with local police. Of course, this would also mean that police would need additional training (such as the work International Justice Mission does) to help stop trafficking.

The third step in eradicating human trafficking lies with businesses and business owners who must take the lead in ending labor trafficking. For example, "Bettys & Taylors of Harrogate (United Kingdom), a traditional family business specializing in

5   Susan Abram, "Prostitution in Los Angeles: Programs like Children of the Night are all too rare," *Los Angeles Daily News*, May 8, 2014, http://www.dailynews.com/social-affairs/20140518/prostitution-in-los-angeles-programs-like-children-of-the-night-are-all-too-rare.

6   Aronowitz et al., "Analyzing the Business Model," 59

7   Siddarth Kara, *Sex Trafficking: Inside the Business of Modern Slavery*" (New York: Columbia University Press, 2009), Kindle edition.

coffees and teas, have ... trained their buyers as social auditors."[8] Their buyers, when visiting farms, are alert to signs of trafficking, making sure that workers are humanely treated and fairly compensated.

The Global Business Coalition Against Human Trafficking (gBCAT) was formed to help large corporations recognize and respond to issues surrounding human trafficking. With companies such as Ford Motor and Coca-Cola as members, gBCAT works to eliminate labor trafficking from global supply chains and to combat sex trafficking (primarily in the travel and tourism industries.)[9] For example, Coca-Cola now uses third-party audits of their supply chains in order to remain accountable. Voluntary private programs are an immense help in combating trafficking.

Financial institutions are also finding ways to end trafficking. It is imperative that banks that see the money from trafficking flow in and out are included in the legal process to stop traffickers. Lisa Anderson at Reuters explains:

> [Manhattan] District Attorney Cyrus R. Vance, Jr. said a partnership between institutions such as JPMorgan Chase, Western Union and Bank of America and law enforcement to share data on client transactions was starting to pay dividends.
>
> "I think we have stepped up our game," Vance told the Thomson Reuters Foundation.
>
> A speaker at the opening of the foundation's third annual Trust Women conference ... Vance said data, such as that produced by the initiative, has led to twenty-two

---

8   Aronowitz et al., "Analyzing the Business Model," 71

9   gBCAT, "About gBCAT," accessed November 19, 2014, http://www.gbcat.org/index.html#about.

> ongoing sex trafficking investigations and contributed to several trials and convictions.[10]

This initiative will be expanding to the European Union, with the hope of garnering success there as well. Bank employees are trained to look for red flags:

> regular transfer of funds from employee accounts back to the employer's account, cross-border transfer of funds inconsistent with the stated business purpose of the client and recurrent business transactions taking place at odd hours and for suspiciously large amounts of money.
>
> For example, experts said, a nail salon putting through a charge for $300 at 2 a.m. is probably providing more than a manicure/pedicure.[11]

Strengthening the rule of law, the fourth step toward eradicating human trafficking in the developing world, is clearly necessary. There is no way around this essential yet time-consuming task. It is not glamorous work; it does not attract celebrity endorsements or television specials with actors manning the phones. It is dull and difficult work, but it is dull and difficult work that will save lives.

Would Legalizing Prostitution Help?

We must pause here to examine one common argument for reducing sex trafficking: legalizing prostitution. Some argue that, with the legalization of selling and buying sex, prostitutes

---

[10] Lisa Anderson, "US Data War on Sex Trafficking to Reach Europe," (paper presented to the Thompson Reuters Foundation, Trust Women conference, Reuters.com, November 18, 2014), http://www.reuters.com/article/2014/11/18/women-conference-vance-idUSL6N0T74AB20141118.

[11] Anderson, "US Data War on Sex Trafficking."

will have legal protection, the health of "sex workers" could be regulated, and corruption surrounding the sex industry could be tamed.

Melissa Farley, a clinical psychologist and founding director of San Francisco's Prostitution Research & Education, is firmly against the legalization of prostitution.

> Prostitution is a commodified form of violence against women, a last-ditch survival option rather than a job choice. The lies that prostitution is a victimless crime, that she chose it, or even that prostitution isn't really happening at all—enable people to avoid the discomfort of knowing about the brutal realities of prostitution. And sex businesses rely on social, political and legal denial of … the harms of prostitution.
>
> In prostitution, johns and pimps transform certain women and girls into objects for sexual use. Many research studies provide evidence for the harms caused by this process. The emotional consequences of prostitution are the same in widely varying cultures whether it's high or low class, legal or illegal, in a brothel, a strip club, a massage parlor, or [on] the street.[12]

Legalizing prostitution would be akin to legalized slavery or legalized child abuse. It strips the person of their innate dignity and objectifies them. As Saint Augustine said, "An unjust law is no law at all." Legalizing prostitution would be a glaring injustice.

---

[12] Melissa Farley, "Prostitution, Liberalism and Slavery," *Logos: A Journal of Modern Society & Culture*, accessed November 19, 2014, http://prostitutionresearch.com/wp-content/uploads/2014/02/Prostitution-Liberalism-and-Slavery_Melissa-Farley-2013.pdf.

The Private Sector and the Elimination of Human Trafficking

The fifth method to eradicate human trafficking involves the Catholic social teaching of *subsidiarity*, which means that those closest to a problem respond to it, as long as they are capable of doing so. Smaller and less complex entities are far better equipped to deal with local issues than are larger and more complex organizations. For example, parents are the best authorities regarding their children's behavior, which means that we, as parents, do not give a government the authority to handle "time-outs" for our toddlers. The hungry among us should normally be fed by individuals and organizations in our communities, not by a federal agency. Those closest to the problem are most familiar with it. The needs of the hungry and homeless in Detroit are different from those in Des Moines or New Delhi. The private sector is far more efficient than any government entity. Just as imperatively, subsidiarity limits the reach of government and protects individual liberty.

Subsidiarity is a good guide for both eliminating human trafficking and caring for its victims. Private local agencies with "boots on the ground" are far more able to work with at-risk communities, victims, and survivors. While human trafficking is a global phenomenon, labor trafficking in Bangkok is not the same as it is in Boise, and the needs of an adult survivor are very different from those of a child. Unwieldy government programs with "blanket" policies simply are not agile enough to meet the unique needs of every community (let alone individuals), nor are they able to quickly and competently coordinate with other governments.

One organization that does subsidiarity very well is Women At Risk, International (WAR, International) based in Grand Rapids, Michigan. This organization has programs and partners in over forty countries and provides help for those caught up in human trafficking. From educational programs and orphanages aimed at keeping young people from becoming victims, to emergency safe houses for those escaping trafficking situations, to microenterprise programs that allow survivors to create lives of hope and fulfillment for themselves, WAR, International is a powerful example of the good that can be done by private citizens and local agencies.

Chloe survived human trafficking. She found a place to both heal and move forward at a WAR, International safe house that teaches women to make specialty beauty care products.

> Making sugar scrubs has been a source of peace for Chloe, a child caught in a nightmare and desperate to survive. Sold by her father [to traffickers] … Chloe is a teenage domestic trafficking victim … As she makes her sugar scrub, Chloe is not only working through her past, but she is also building into her future. The funds that come from sugar scrub sales helped Chloe complete her online high school education as she was in hiding with her mother.[13]

WAR, International's website says their goal is to educate communities about risk issues and provide individuals with practical ways to assist in eradicating trafficking, as well as to "empower survivors to live and work with dignity and hope."[14] This model—education, prevention, survival, and empowerment—is an excellent one for fighting human trafficking.

The Role of Religious Institutions

The sixth method for eradicating human trafficking lies with the world's major religions because they possess a key element

---

[13] "Chloe," Women At Risk, International, accessed October 13, 2014, http://warinternational.org/stories-of-women/chloe/.

[14] Women At Risk, International, accessed November 20, 2014, http://warinternational.org/.

that puts them one step ahead in the fight: They have a global presence.

Religious institutions already have networks in place that are being used to battle trafficking. In December 2014, Orthodox, Anglican, Jewish, Muslim, Buddhist, and Hindu representatives met at the Vatican with Pope Francis to sign an interfaith declaration regarding trafficking. The declaration reads in part:

> Modern slavery, in terms of human trafficking, forced labour and prostitution, organ trafficking, and any relationship that fails to respect the fundamental conviction that all people are equal and have the same freedom and dignity, is a crime against humanity. We pledge ourselves here today to do all in our power, within our faith communities and beyond, to work together for the freedom of all those who are enslaved and trafficked so that their future may be restored. Today we have the opportunity, awareness, wisdom, innovation and technology to achieve this human and moral imperative.[15]

Lord Griffiths has said that there is no need to create new global organizations in order to deal with problems such as trafficking because religious institutions already possess the necessary resources. It is easy to see challenges in our modern world as purely secular, with purely secular antidotes, but that is both wrong and counterproductive. "The Church," Griffiths says, "is a witness to [Christ's] kingdom and because of that has great potential to influence our world for the better."[16] He

---

[15] "Crimes Against Humanity," L'Osservatore Romano, December 2, 2014, http://www.osservatoreromano.va/en/news/crimes-against-humanity.

[16] Lord Griffiths of Fforestfach, *Globalization, Poverty, and International Development: Insights from* Centesimus Annus (Grand Rapids: Acton Institute, 2012), Kindle edition.

reminds us that, for Christians, justice is not merely a matter of the rules being fairly applied in a game, but about those who cannot play the game, or those who get injured in the game. Justice, for Christians, is about the good of all, each individual, not a conglomerate or a few successful individuals. With this moral underpinning, the Church is uniquely suited for combating human trafficking.

In addition, the Church has a universal network of care already in place. Nathalie Lummert is the director of programs for migration and refugee services for the United States Conference of Catholic Bishops (USCCB). In April 2014, Lummert testified before a US Congressional subcommittee regarding the efficacy of the Church's work regarding trafficking. She gave three reasons why faith-based organizations have peerless traits when fighting trafficking.

First, Lummert points out that faith-based organizations "act from a theological and philosophical perspective"[17] and commitment to such principles creates an urgency to respond among believers. Second, the universality of many faith-based organizations "enhance[s] their capacity to give voice and volume to the cry for justice." Third, faith-based organizations have resources, both human and financial, working in an established infrastructure that would be doing this work regardless of any government urging, in response to the "moral gravity of the issue and the ongoing suffering of its victims."

---

[17] Nathalie Lummert, "Effective Accountability: Tier Rankings in the Fight Against Human Trafficking" (testimony before a US Congressional Subcommittee regarding the efficacy of the Church's work regarding trafficking, USCCB, April 29, 2014), 13, http://www.usccb.org/about/migration-policy/upload/Trafficking-TIP-Report-Testimony-FINALAP.pdf.

Ending Trafficking

The zeal of the abolitionists—men and women such as Frederick Douglass, Harriet Beecher Stowe, and William Wilberforce—must be the zeal with which we undertake the task of ending human trafficking.

On the twenty-fourth anniversary of the signing of the Emancipation Proclamation, Douglass proclaimed:

> Where justice is denied, where poverty is enforced, where ignorance prevails, and where any one class is made to feel that society is an organized conspiracy to oppress, rob and degrade them, neither persons nor property will be safe.[18]

While Douglass could not have foreseen the likes of sex tourism in Thailand or the global scale of labor trafficking, his intimate knowledge of the horrors we humans can visit upon each other (man's inhumanity to man) makes his voice as emphatic as ever.

---

[18] Frederick Douglass, Center for Economic and Social Justice, "Quotes Collection: Wisdom from the Just Third Way," accessed November 20, 2014, http://www.cesj.org/resources/reference-tools/quotes-collection/.

Appendix

Recognizing the Signs of Human Trafficking

Common Work and Living Conditions: The Individual(s) in Question

- Is not free to leave or come and go as he or she wishes
- Is under eighteen and is providing commercial sex acts
- Is in the commercial sex industry and has a pimp/manager
- Is unpaid, paid very little, or paid only through tips
- Works excessively long and/or unusual hours
- Is not allowed breaks or suffers under unusual restrictions at work
- Owes a large debt and is unable to pay it off
- Was recruited through false promises concerning the nature and conditions of his or her work
- High security measures exist in the work and/or living locations (e.g., opaque windows, boarded up windows, bars on windows, barbed wire, security cameras, and so forth)

Poor Mental Health or Abnormal Behavior: The Individual(s) in Question

- Is fearful, anxious, depressed, submissive, tense, or nervous/paranoid
- Exhibits unusually fearful or anxious behavior after bringing up law enforcement
- Avoids eye contact

Poor Physical Health: The Individual(s) in Question

- Lacks health care
- Appears malnourished
- Shows signs of physical and/or sexual abuse, physical restraint, confinement, or torture

Lack of Control: The Individual(s) in Question

- Has few or no personal possessions
- Is not in control of his or her own money, has no financial records, or has no bank account
- Is not in control of his or her own identification documents (ID or passport)
- Is not allowed or able to speak for themselves (a third party may insist on being present and/or translating)

Other

- Claims to be just visiting and inability to clarify where he or she is staying or address
- Lack of knowledge of whereabouts and/or do not know what city he or she is in
- Loss of sense of time
- Has numerous inconsistencies in his or her story

This list is not exhaustive and represents only a selection of possible indicators. Furthermore, the red flags in this list may not be present in all trafficking cases and are not cumulative. (Source: Polaris Project)

To request help or report suspected human trafficking, call the National Human Trafficking Resource Center hotline at 1-888-373-7888, or text INFO or HELP to: BeFree (233733). (US only.)

Acton Institute Core Principles

Dignity of the Person—The human person, created in the image of God, is individually unique, rational, the subject of moral agency, and a co-creator. Accordingly, he possesses intrinsic value and dignity, implying certain rights and duties both for himself and other persons. These truths about the dignity of the human person are known through revelation, but they are also discernible through reason.

Social Nature of the Person—Although persons find ultimate fulfillment only in communion with God, one essential aspect of the development of persons is our social nature and capacity to act for disinterested ends. The person is fulfilled by interacting with other persons and by participating in moral goods. There are voluntary relations of exchange, such as market transactions that realize economic value. These transactions may give rise to moral value as well. There are also voluntary relationships of mutual dependence such as promises, friendships, marriages, and the family—which are moral goods. These, too, may have other sorts of values such as religious, economic, aesthetic, and so forth.

Importance of Social Institutions—Because persons are by nature social, various human persons develop social institutions. The institutions of civil society, especially the family, are the primary sources of a society's moral culture. These social institutions are neither created by nor derive their legitimacy from the state. The state must respect their autonomy and provide the support necessary to ensure the free and orderly operation of all social institutions in their respective spheres.

Human Action—Humans are by nature acting persons. Through human action, the person can actualize his or her potentiality by freely choosing the moral goods that fulfill his or her nature.

Sin—Although human beings in their created nature are good, in their current state, they are fallen and corrupted by sin. The reality of sin makes the state necessary to restrain evil. The ubiquity of sin, however, requires that the state be limited in its power and jurisdiction. The persistent reality of sin requires that we be skeptical of all utopian "solutions" to social ills such as poverty and injustice.

Rule of Law and the Subsidiary Role of Government—The government's primary responsibility is to promote the common good, that is, to maintain the rule of law, and to preserve basic duties and rights. The government's role is not to usurp free actions, but to minimize those conflicts that may arise when the free actions of persons and social institutions result in competing interests. The state should exercise this responsibility according to the principle of subsidiarity. This principle has two components: First, jurisdictionally broader institutions must refrain from usurping the proper functions that should be performed by the person and institutions more immediate to him or to her. Second, jurisdictionally broader institutions should assist individual persons and institutions more immediate to the person only when the latter cannot fulfill their proper functions.

Creation of Wealth—Material impoverishment undermines the conditions that allow humans to flourish. The best means of reducing poverty is to protect private property rights through the rule of law. This allows people to enter into voluntary exchange circles in which to express their creative nature. Wealth is created when human beings creatively transform matter into resources. Because human beings can create wealth, economic exchange need not be a zero-sum game.

Economic Liberty—Liberty, in a positive sense, is achieved by fulfilling one's nature as a person by freely choosing to do what one ought. Economic liberty is a species of liberty so-stated. As such, the bearer of economic liberty not only has certain rights, but also duties. An economically free person, for example, must be free to enter the market voluntarily. Hence, those who have the power to interfere with the market are not only duty bound to remove any artificial barrier to entry in the market but also to protect private and shared property rights. The economically free person will also bear the duty to others to participate in the market as a moral agent and in accordance with moral goods. Therefore, the law must guarantee private property rights and voluntary exchange.

Economic Value—In economic theory, economic value is subjective because its existence depends on it being felt by a subject. Economic value is the significance that a subject attaches to a thing whenever he perceives a causal connection between this thing and the satisfaction of a present, urgent want. The subject may be wrong in his value judgment by attributing value to a thing that will not or cannot satisfy his present, urgent want. The truth of economic value judgments is settled just in case that thing can satisfy the expected want. While this does not imply the realization of any other sort of value, something can have both subjective economic value and objective moral value.

Priority of Culture—Liberty flourishes in a society supported by a moral culture that embraces the truth about the transcendent origin and destiny of the human person. This moral culture leads to harmony and to the proper ordering of society. While the various institutions within the political, economic, and other spheres are important, the family is the primary inculcator of the moral culture in a society.

References

Abram, Susan. "Prostitution in Los Angeles: Programs Like Children of the Night Are All Too Rare." *Los Angeles Daily News*, May 18, 2014. Available at http://www.dailynews.com/social-affairs/20140518/prostitution-in-los-angeles-programs-like-children-of-the-night-are-all-too-rare.

Acton Institute. "Acton Institute Core Principles." Accessed November 14, 2014. http://www.acton.org/about/acton-institute-core-principles.

Anderson, Lisa. "US Data War on Sex Trafficking to Reach Europe." Reuters. November 18, 2014. http://www.reuters.com/article/2014/11/18/women-conference-vance-idUSL6N0T-74AB20141118.

Anti-Slavery International. "Slavery on the High Street: Forced Labour in the Manufacture of Garments for International Brands." June 2012. http://www.antislavery.org/includes/documents/cm_docs/2012/s/1_slavery_on_the_high_street_june_2012_final.pdf.

Apparent Project. "Job Creation." Accessed November 6, 2014. http://www.apparentproject.org/job-creation/4575497652.

Aronowitz, Alexis A. *Human Trafficking, Human Misery.* Kindle edition. Westport, CT: Praeger, 2009.

Aronowitz, Alexis, Gerda Theuermann, and Elena Tyurykanova. *Analysing the Business Model of Trafficking in Human Beings to Better Prevent the Crime*. Organization for Security and Co-operation in Europe (OSCE). September 30, 2010. http://www.osce.org/cthb/69028.

BBC News. "Cellar Slave Girl: Salford Couple Must Pay Victim £100,000." October 15, 2014. http://www.bbc.com/news/uk-england-manchester-29559771.

Bechard, Raymond. "What You Must Know About the 'Deep Web.'" Examiner.com. April 25, 2014. http://www.examiner.com/article/what-you-must-know-about-the-deep-web.

Belz, Mindy. "From the Work of Their Hands." *WORLD maga-zine*. February 22, 2014. http://www.worldmag.com/2014/02/from_the_work_of_their_hands.

Benedict XVI (Pope). 2009. *Caritas in Veritate*.

Brienzo, Andy. "Trafficking for Organ Trade: The Often-Overlooked Form of Human Trafficking." *Human Trafficking Center Blog*. June 18, 2014. http://humantraffickingcenter.org/posts-by-htc-associates/trafficking-organ-trade-often-overlooked-form-human-trafficking/.

Brienzo, Andy, and Jonathan Hudlow. 2014. "Fighting Human Trafficking through Transit Monitoring: A Data Driven Model." Interdisciplinary Conference on Human Trafficking. University of Nebraska-Lincoln. Available at http://humantrafficking.unl.edu/program.aspx.

Chinery-Hesse, Herman. "Business vs. Aid & Charity." PovertyCure.org. Accessed October 29, 2014. http://www.povertycure.org/voices/herman-chinery-hesse/.

Chuan, Janie. "Beyond a Snapshot: Preventing Human Trafficking in the Global Economy." *Indiana Journal of Global Legal Studies*. January 2006. http://www.repository.law.indiana.edu/ijgls/vol13/iss1/5/.

COATNET. "Caritas Internationalis Commitment on Trafficking." October 2005. http://www.caritas.org/includes/pdf/coatnet/CI_Commitment-2.pdf.

Coffey, John. "The Abolition of the Slave Trade: Christian Conscience and Political Action." *Jubilee Centre Biblical Thinking for Public Life*. Accessed October 1, 2014. http://www.jubilee-centre.org/the-abolition-of-the-slave-trade-christian-conscience-and-political-action-by-john-coffey/.

Dank, Meredith, et al. 2014. *Estimating the Size and Structure of the Underground Commercial Sex Economy in Eight Major US Cities*. Urban Institute.

Douglass, Frederick. Center for Economic and Social Justice. "Quotes Collection: Wisdom from the Just Third Way." Accessed November 20, 2014. http://www.cesj.org/resources/reference-tools/quotes-collection/.

Elam, Jerome. "The Story of One. Vandalized Innocence: The Story of Trafficked Boys Hidden in Plain Sight." Communities Digital News (CDN). September 14, 2014. http://www.commdiginews.com/life/trafficked-boys-vandalized-innocence-hidden-in-plain-sight-26356/#AbLL85mMbRRrMcxy.99.

Farley, Melissa. "Prostitution, Liberalism, and Slavery." *Logos: A Journal of Modern Society and Culture*. Accessed January 4, 2015. http://logosjournal.com/2013/farley/.

Farrell, Amy, et al. *Identifying Challenges to Improve the Investigation and Prosecution of State and Local Human Trafficking Cases Executive Summary*. Washington, DC: National Institute of Justice, 2012.

Finnis, John, *Natural Law and Natural Rights* (Oxford: Clarendon Press, 1980).

Fletcher, Anna. "Human Trafficking within the Human Global Supply Chain." *Sigma Iota Rho Journal of International Business*. April 30, 2014.

Free the Slaves. "About Slavery: Slavery in History." Accessed October 17, 2014. https://www.freetheslaves.net/SlaveryinHistory.

gBCAT. Accessed November 19, 2014. http://www.gbcat.org/index. html#about.

Gelles, Richard J., and Staci Perlman, *Estimated Annual Cost of Child Abuse and Neglect* (Chicago: Prevent Child Abuse America, 2012).

Griffiths of Fforestfach, Lord Brian. *Globalization, Poverty, and International Development: Insights from Centesimus Annus.* Grand Rapids: Acton Institute, 2012.

"Haiti, U.S. State Department Trafficking in Persons Report," June 2014.

Horvat II, John. The American Society for the Defense of Tradition, Family and Property, "Interview with Dr. Samuel Gregg: 'Culture Drives History, Societies and Economic Life,'" July 28, 2014, http://www.tfp.org/tfp-home/news-commentary/interview-with-dr-samuel-gregg-culture-drives-history-societies-and-economic-life.html.

International Cocoa Organization. "The Chocolate Industry." February 4, 2014. http://www.icco.org/about-cocoa/chocolate-industry.html.

International Justice Mission. *Justice Review: A Journal on Protection and Justice for the Poor, 2014–2015.* September 2014.

International Labour Organization (ILO): Geneva. "Profits and Poverty: The Economics of Forced Labour." May 20, 2014. http://www.ilo.org/wcmsp5/groups/public/---ed_norm/---declaration/documents/publication/wcms_243391.pdf.

John Paul II. Letter of John Paul II to Archbishop Jean-Louis Tauran on the Occasion of the International Conference "Twenty-First Century Slavery—The Human Rights Dimension to Trafficking in Human Beings." Vatican City: Vatican.va, May 15, 2002. http://www.vatican.va/holy_father/john_paul_ii/letters/2002/documents/hf_jp-ii_let_20020515_tauran_en.html.

Johnson, C. Neal, "Spiritual & Social Aspects of Business." "Voices." Interview with PovertyCure. Accessed November 5, 2014. http://www.povertycure.org/voices/c-neal-johnson/.

Kara, Siddarth. *Sex Trafficking: Inside the Business of Modern Slavery.* New York: Columbia University Press, 2009. Kindle edition.

Kessler, Mike. "Gone Girls: Human Trafficking on the Home Front." *Los Angeles Magazine.* Los Angeles, October 14, 2014.

Labor Law Center Blog. "California Company Convicted of Slavery and Human Trafficking." August 7, 2007. http://blog.laborlawcenter.com/news/california-company-convicted-of-slavery-and-human-trafficking/.

Lincoln, Abraham. *The Emancipation Proclamation.* National Archives and Records Administration: Featured Documents. January 1, 1863. Accessed October 15, 2014. http://www.archives.gov/exhibits/featured_documents/emancipation_proclamation/transcript.html.

Lummert, Nathalie, interview by Global Health, Global Human Rights and International Organizations on Effective Accountability: Tier Rankings in the Fight Against Human Trafficking U.S. Subcommittee on Africa. *Director, Special Programs, Migration and Refugee Services/U.S. Conference of Catholic Bishops* (April 29, 2014).

Malarek, Victor. *The Johns: Sex for Sale and the Men Who Buy It.* Toronto: Key Porter Books, 2010.

McKenzie, David. "The Human Cost of Chocolate." *The CNN Freedom Project: Ending Modern Slavery.* January 16, 2012. http://thecnnfreedomproject.blogs.cnn.com/2012/01/16/chocolate-explainer/.

Michigan Commission on Human Trafficking. "2013 Report on Human Trafficking."

Misra, Tanvi. "How the Crime of Labor Trafficking Helps Cities Run." *City Lab.* October 21, 2014. http://www/citylab.com/

crime/2014/10/how-the-crime-of-labor-trafficking-helps-cities-run-381709.

"National Council of Jewish Women and Polaris Join Forces to Raise Awareness about Human Trafficking." *National Council of Jewish Women.* October 28, 2014. http://www.ncjw.org/content_11240.cfm?navID=218.

National Council of Jewish Women (NCJW). "NCJW Condemns Human Trafficking." December 6, 2005. http://www.ncjw.org/content_3137.cfm.

"Norway's Closely Watched Prostitution Ban Works, Study Finds." *Reuters.* August 11, 2014. http://uk.reuters.com/article/2014/08/11/us-norway-prostitution-idUKKBN0GB1BL20140811?irpc=932.

Okeowo, Alexis. "Freedom Fighter." *The New Yorker.* September 8, 2014.

Phelps, Carissa. *Runaway Girl: Escaping Life on the Streets.* New York: Viking, 2012. Kindle edition.

Pope Francis. "Pope Francis: Human Trafficking Is a Crime Against Humanity." News.va. April 10, 2014. Accessed October 2014. http://www.news.va/en/news/pope-francis-human-trafficking-an-open-wound-on-so.

"Recipe for Ending Poverty: Think, Then Act." Zenit. November 30, 2009. http://www.zenit.org/en/articles/recipe-for-ending-poverty-think-then-act (accessed October 23, 2014).

Polaris Project. "Recognizing the Signs." Accessed November 18, 2014, http://www.polarisproject.org/human-trafficking/recognizing-the-signs.

Rector, Robert, and Rachel Sheffield. "The War on Poverty After 50 Years." The Heritage Foundation. September 15, 2014. http://www.heritage.org/research/reports/2014/09/the-war-on-poverty-after-50-years.

Redlight Traffic. http://www.redlighttraffic.org/.

Saar, Malika Saada. "The Scandal of the Players Ball." The Daily Beast. December 10, 2010. http://www.thedailybeast.com/articles/2010/12/10/players-ball-hip-hop-and-sexual-abuse.html.

Shared Hope International. *Demanding Justice Report 2014.* http://sharedhope.org/wp-content/uploads/2014/08/Demanding_Justice_Report_2014.pdf.

Sirico, Robert A., 2014. "The Moral Case for Business." "Voices." PovertyCure. Accessed November 5, 2014. http://www.povertycure.org/voices/rev-robert-a-sirico/.

Smith, Holly Austin. *Walking Prey: How America's Youth Are Vulnerable to Sex Slavery.* New York: Palgrave-MacMillan, 2014. Kindle edition.

Smith, Linda. "AZ Central—'Why Can't She Run Away?' and Other Nonsense." Shared Hope International. October 10, 2014. http://sharedhope.org/2014/10/10/az-central-why-cant-she-run-away/.

"Sweatshop Free Clothing." World Conscience. http://freeconsciencefashion.tumblr.com/Sweatshopfreeclothing.

"Sweetie." Women at Risk, International. Accessed November 4, 2014. http://warinternational.org/story/sweetie/.

"The High Cost of Cheap Clothes." *Vice News.* October 17, 2014.

Tomkins, Stephen. *William Wilberforce: A Biography.* Grand Rapids: Eerdmans, 2007.

"Towards the End of Poverty." *The Economist.* June 1, 2014. http://www.economist.com/news/leaders/21578665-nearly-1-billion-people-have-been-taken-out-extreme-poverty-20-years-world-should-aim.

United Nations Office on Drugs and Crime. "Human Trafficking." Accessed October 14, 2014. http://www.unodc.org/unodc/en/human-trafficking/what-is-human-trafficking.html.

Urban Institute. "Understanding the Organization, Operation, and Victimization Process of Labor Trafficking in the United States." October 2014. http://www.urban.org/UploadedPDF/413249-Labor-Trafficking-in-the-United-States.pdf.

United States Department of Justice. "Child Exploitation & Obscenity Section." May 17, 2011. Accessed November 7, 2014. http://www.justice.gov/criminal/ceos/subjectareas/prostitution.html.

U.S. Department of State. "Trafficking in Persons Report 2014." Accessed October 23, 2014, http://www.state.gov/j/tip/rls/tiprpt/2014/.

U.S. Immigration and Customs Enforcement. "Continued Presence: Temporary Status for Victims of Human Trafficking." August 2010. http://www.ice.gov/doclib/human-trafficking/pdf/continued-presence.pdf.

"Vatican, Anglicans, Muslims Sign Accord against Human Trafficking." Ecumenism.net. Accessed November 20, 2014. http://ecumenism.net/2014/03/vatican-anglicans-muslims-accord-against-human-trafficking.htm.

Yardley, Jim. "Report on Deadly Factory Collapse in Bangladesh Finds Widespread Blame." *New York Times.* May 22, 2013. http://www.nytimes.com/2013/05/23/world/asia/report-on-bangladesh-building-collapse-finds-widespread-blame.html?_r=0.

Wheaton, Elizabeth M., Edward J. Schauer, and Thomas V. Galli. *Economics of Human Trafficking.* International Organization for Migration. Oxford: Blackwell, 2010.

Works Consulted

Al-Mahmood, et al. "Human Traffickers in Bay of Bengal Cast Sights on Bangladesh." *The Wall Street Journal*. October 28, 2014, http://online.wsj.com/articles/human-traffickers-in-bay-of-bengal-cast-sights-on-bangladesh-1414536642?mod=e2tw.

Belles, Nita. 2011. *In Our Backyard: A Christian Perspective on Human Trafficking in the United States*. Free River.

Bennhold, Katrin. 2014. "Years of Rape and 'Utter Contempt' in Britain." *The New York Times*, September 1.

Better Work. Accessed October 17, 2014. http://betterwork.org/global/.

Bonetti, Sr. Eugenia. "Breaking Down the Chains of Modern-Day Slavery." *Office for Migration Policy: Seminar on Human Trafficking*. Southwark: Migration Office of the Episcopal Conference of Bishops in England and Wales, 2011.

Brewer, Devin. "Globalization and Human Trafficking." *Topical Research Digest: Human Rights and Human Trafficking*.

"Dark Chocolate." Lexis Nexis. 2013. http://www.nexis.co.uk/pdf/Dark_Chocolate.pdf.

Diu, Nisha Lilia. "What the UN Doesn't Want You to Know." *The Telegraph*, February 6, 2012.

Gao, George. "Where People Say Giving Bribes Gets You Ahead in Life." Pew Research Center. October 23, 2014. http://www. pewresearch.org/fact-tank/2014/10/23/where-people-say-giving-bribes-gets-you-ahead-in-life/.

Lindenberg, Adolpho. *The Free Market in a Christian Society.* Washington, DC: St. Antoninus Institute for Catholic Education in Business, 1999.

"Sister Eugenia Bonetti." Robert F. Kennedy Center for Justice & Human Rights. http://rfkcenter.org/sister-eugenia-bonetti.

Sneed, Tierney. "Why Cleaning Up the Fashion Industry Is So Messy." *U.S. News & World Report.* July 26, 2014. http://www.usnews.com/news/articles/2014/07/16/efforts-to-clean-up-fast-fashion-supply-chains-face-a-tough-road.

Talitha Kum: International Network of Consecrated Life Against Trafficking in Persons. http://www.talithakum.info/index.php?lang=1.

The Bloody Yellow House. Accessed October 21, 2014. http://thebloody-ellowhouse.wordpress.com/.

"Veronica's Voice Statistics." *Veronica's Voice.* Accessed October 13, 2014. http://www.veronicasvoice.org/statistics/.

Vulliamy, Ed. "Has the UN Learned Lessons of Bosnian Sex Slavery Revealed in Rachel Weisz Film?" *The Guardian.* January 14, 2012. ttp://www.theguardian.com/world/2012/jan/15/bosnia-sex-trafficking-whistleblower.

About the Author

Elise Graveline Hilton holds a BA in religious studies from Alma College and an MA in world religions from Western Michigan University. After taking time to raise her five children, she returned to the paid workforce a decade ago. As the Communications Specialist for the Acton Institute, she writes regularly at the Acton PowerBlog and speaks on faith, family, and sanctity of life issues.

Made in the USA
Middletown, DE
22 February 2015